Laws and Legislation

REVISITING AND EVALUATING THE CONGRESSIONAL REVIEW ACT

LAWS AND LEGISLATION

State Secrets Protection Act
Lara H. Nellington
2009 ISBN: 978-1-60692-711-3

Revisiting and Evaluating the Congressional Review Act
Katherine R. Williamson
2009 ISBN: 978-1-60692-687-1

Laws and Legislation

Revisiting and Evaluating the Congressional Review Act

Katherine R. Williamson
Editor

Nova Science Publishers, Inc.
New York

For permission to use material from this book please contact us:
Telephone 631-231-7269; Fax 631-231-8175
Web Site: http://www.novapublishers.com

LIBRARY OF CONGRESS CATALOGING-IN-PUBLICATION DATA
Available upon request.
ISBN: 978-1-60692-687-1

Published by Nova Science Publishers, Inc. ✢ New York

CONTENTS

PREFACE

This year marks the 10th anniversary of the Congressional Review Act (CRA). Congressional oversight of rulemaking using the CRA can be an important and useful tool for monitoring the regulatory process and balancing and accommodating the concerns of American citizens and businesses with the effects of federal agencies' rules. This statement provides an overview of the purpose and provisions of CRA; GAO's role and activities in fulfilling its responsibilities under the Act; and trends on CRA within the broader context of developments in presidential and congressional oversight of federal agencies' rulemaking.

Chapter 1 - On March 29, 1996, the President signed into law the Small Business Regulatory Enforcement Fairness Act of 1996 (SBREFA), P.L. 104-121, 110 Stat. 857-874, Subtitle E of which for the first time established a mechanism by which Congress can review and disapprove, by means of an expedited legislative process, virtually all federal agency rules. However, critics have questioned the efficacy of the review scheme as a vehicle to control agency rulemaking through the exercise of legislative oversight. These questions have been raised despite the use of the CRA to nullify OSHA's controversial ergonomics standards in March 2001. In the view of some observers, the OSHA action was the result of a unique confluence of circumstances not likely to soon recur: the White House and both Houses of Congress in the hands of the same political party, a contentious rule promulgated in the waning days of an outgoing Administration; longstanding opposition to the rule by some in Congress and by a broad coalition of business interests; and encouragement of repeal by the President. On the other hand, some maintain that a number of major rules have been affected by the Agency recognition of the existence of the review mechanism, and argue that the review scheme has had a significant influence.

Critics argue that potential impediments to the law's use, the scheme provides no expedited consideration procedure in the House of Representatives; there is no screening mechanism to identify rules that may require special congressional attention; and a disapproval resolution of a significant or politically sensitive rule is likely to need a supermajority to be successful if control of the White House and the Congress are in different political hands, as was the case between April 1996 and January 2001, and is the case now. Moreover, a number of critical interpretive issues remain to be resolved, including the scope of the provisions' coverage of rules; whether an agency failure to report a covered rule is subject to court review and sanction; whether a joint resolution of disapproval may be utilized to veto parts of a rule or only may be directed at the rule in its entirety; and what is the scope of the limitation that precludes an agency from promulgating a "substantially similar" rule after disapproval of a rule. Of a total of 47 joint resolutions of disapproval that have been introduced to date since April 1996, only one has passed and that one may have been sui generis because of the unique circumstances accompanying its passage. During that period some 47,540 major and non-major rules have been reported and become effective.

This chapter will provide a brief explanation of how the structure of the review scheme was expected to operate and describes how it has in fact been utilized. The possible reasons for the relatively limited use of the formal mechanism thus far are assessed.

Chapter 2 - The State Children's Health Insurance Program (SCHIP) finances health care to low-income, uninsured children whose family incomes exceed the eligibility limits under their state's Medicaid program, but who cannot afford other health insurance coverage. To participate in SCHIP, a state must submit a plan that describes how its program meets applicable requirements and must receive approval of the plan from CMS. States are required to amend their plans to reflect changes in federal law, regulation, or policy, and changes in the operation of their programs, including, for example, changes in eligibility criteria or benefits.

Chapter 3 - The definition of "rule" in the Congressional Review Act incorporates by reference the definition of "rule" in the Administrative Procedure Act (APA), with some exceptions. The APA definition of rule includes three elements relevant to GAO's consideration of the SCHIP letter: an agency statement is a rule if it is of general applicability; of future effect; and designed to implement, interpret, or prescribe law or policy. GAO concluded that the letter meets these criteria and that none of the exceptions in the Review Act apply. GAO found the letter to be of general applicability since it extends to all states that seek to enroll children with effective family incomes exceeding 250 percent of the FPL in their SCHIP programs, as well as to states that have already enrolled such children. In addition, GAO found it to be of future effect, that is, concerned with policy considerations for the future rather than the evaluation of past or present conduct. Finally, GAO found that the letter is designed to implement, interpret, or prescribe law or policy since it purports to clarify and explain the manner in which CMS applies statutory and regulatory requirements to states that want to extend coverage under their SCHIP programs to children with effective family incomes above 250 percent of the FPL and seeks to promote the implementation of statutory requirements applicable to state plans.

Chapter 4 - CRA gives Congress an opportunity to review most rules before they take effect and to disapprove those found to be too burdensome, excessive, inappropriate, duplicative, or otherwise objectionable. Under CRA, two types of rules, major and nonmajor, must be submitted to both Houses of Congress and GAO before they can take effect. The Office of Information and Regulatory Affairs (OIRA) of the Office of Management and Budget specifies which rules are designated as major rules based on criteria set out in the CRA. Major rules cannot be effective until 60 days after publication in the *Federal Register* or submission to Congress and GAO, whichever is later. Congress may disapprove agencies' rules by introducing a resolution of disapproval that, if adopted by both Houses of Congress and signed by the President, can nullify an agency's rule. Members of Congress seldom have attempted to use this process.

In: Revisiting and Evaluating the Congressional... ISBN: 978-1-60692-687-1
Editor: K. R. Williamson, pp. 1-58

Chapter 1

CONGRESSIONAL REVIEW OF AGENCY RULEMAKING: AN UPDATE AND ASSESSMENT OF THE CONGRESSIONAL REVIEW ACT AFTER A DECADE*

Morton Rosenberg

ABSTRACT

On March 29, 1996, the President signed into law the Small Business Regulatory Enforcement Fairness Act of 1996 (SBREFA), P.L. 104-121, 110 Stat. 857-874, Subtitle E of which for the first time established a mechanism by which Congress can review and disapprove, by means of an expedited legislative process, virtually all federal agency rules. However, critics have questioned the efficacy of the review scheme as a vehicle to control agency rulemaking through the exercise of legislative oversight. These questions have been raised despite the use of the CRA to nullify OSHA's controversial ergonomics standards in March 2001. In the view of some observers, the OSHA action was the result of a unique confluence of circumstances not likely to soon recur: the White House and both Houses of Congress in the hands of the same political party, a contentious rule promulgated in the waning days of an outgoing Administration; longstanding opposition to the rule by some in Congress and by a broad coalition of

---

* This is an edited, excerpted and augmented edition of a Congressional Research Service publication, Report RL30116, dated May 8, 2008.

business interests; and encouragement of repeal by the President. On the other hand, some maintain that a number of major rules have been affected by the Agency recognition of the existence of the review mechanism, and argue that the review scheme has had a significant influence.

Critics argue that potential impediments to the law's use, the scheme provides no expedited consideration procedure in the House of Representatives; there is no screening mechanism to identify rules that may require special congressional attention; and a disapproval resolution of a significant or politically sensitive rule is likely to need a supermajority to be successful if control of the White House and the Congress are in different political hands, as was the case between April 1996 and January 2001, and is the case now. Moreover, a number of critical interpretive issues remain to be resolved, including the scope of the provisions' coverage of rules; whether an agency failure to report a covered rule is subject to court review and sanction; whether a joint resolution of disapproval may be utilized to veto parts of a rule or only may be directed at the rule in its entirety; and what is the scope of the limitation that precludes an agency from promulgating a "substantially similar" rule after disapproval of a rule. Of a total of 47 joint resolutions of disapproval that have been introduced to date since April 1996, only one has passed and that one may have been sui generis because of the unique circumstances accompanying its passage. During that period some 47,540 major and non-major rules have been reported and become effective.

This chapter will provide a brief explanation of how the structure of the review scheme was expected to operate and describes how it has in fact been utilized. The possible reasons for the relatively limited use of the formal mechanism thus far are assessed.

INTRODUCTION

On March 29, 1996, the President signed into law the Small Business Regulatory Enforcement Fairness Act of 1996 (SBREFA), P.L. 104-121, 110 Stat. 857-874, Subtitle E of which for the first time established a mechanism by which Congress can review and disapprove, by means of an expedited legislative process, virtually all federal agency rules. This was part of the Contract with America. Critics have questioned the efficacy of the review scheme as a vehicle to control agency rulemaking through the exercise of legislative oversight. These questions have been raised despite the use of the CRA to nullify OSHA's controversial ergonomics standard in March 2001. It has been argued that the action on the OSHA proposal was the result of a unique confluence of circumstances not likely to soon recur: the White House and both Houses of Congress in the hands of the same political party, a contentious rule promulgated in the waning days of an outgoing Administration;

longstanding opposition to the rule by some in Congress and by a broad coalition of business interests; and encouragement of repeal by the President. On the other hand, some maintain that a number of major rules have been affected by Agency recognition of the availability of the review mechanism, and argue that the review scheme has had a significant influence.

Critics who maintain that the CRA has not been appropriately utilized assert that the current procedure provides for no expedited consideration in the House of Representatives; lacks a screening mechanism to identify rules that may require special congressional attention; and, that a disapproval resolution of a significant or politically sensitive rule is likely to need a supermajority to be successful if control of the White House and the Congress are in different political hands. They further contend that a number of critical interpretive issues and questions remain to be resolved, including the scope of the provisions' coverage of rules; whether an agency failure to report a covered rule is subject to court review and sanction; whether a joint resolution of disapproval may be utilized to veto parts of a rule or only may be directed at the rule in its entirety; and what is the scope of the limitation that precludes an agency from promulgating a "substantially similar" rule after disapproval of a rule. From these critics' perspective potential impediments and uncertainties have contributed to the fact that of a total of 47 joint resolutions of disapproval that have been introduced to date since April 1996, only one has passed. They point out that during that period over 47,540 major and non-major rules have been reported and become effective.

This chapter will provide a brief explanation of how the review scheme was expected to operate and describe how it has been utilized. The possible reasons for the relatively limited use of the formal review mechanism thus far are assessed.

Many do not support increased utilization of the CRA review process. Those holding this opinion may represent a number of views including concern that expanded use of the process will lead to the disproportionate influence on Federal regulations by powerful interest groups or that many regulations have become too technical to be judged by "non-experts." However, since these positions have seldom been articulated publicly, the are not well represented in this chapter.

REVIEW OF AGENCY RULES

The congressional review mechanism, codified at 5 U.S.C. 801-808, and popularly known as the Congressional Review Act (CRA), requires that all agencies promulgating a covered rule must submit a report to each House of Congress and to the Comptroller General (CG) that contains a copy of the rule, a concise general statement describing the rule (including whether it is deemed to be a major rule), and the proposed effective date of the rule. A covered rule cannot take effect if the report is not submitted. Section 801(a)(1)(A). Each House must send a copy of the report to the chairman and ranking minority member of each jurisdictional committee. Section 801(a)(1)(C). In addition, the promulgating agency must submit to the CG (1) a complete copy of any cost-benefit analysis; (2) a description of the agency's actions pursuant to the requirements of the Regulatory Flexibility Act and the Unfunded Mandates Reform Act of 1995; and (3) any other relevant information required under any other act or executive order. Such information must also be made "available" to each House. Section 801(a)(1)(B).

Section 804(3) adopts the definition of "rule" found at 5 U.S.C. 55 1(4) which provides that the term rule "means the whole or part of an agency statement of general . . . applicability and future effect designed to implement, interpret, or prescribe law or policy."[1] The legislative history of Section 551(4) indicates that the term is to be broadly construed: "The definition of rule is not limited to substantive rules, but embraces interpretive, organizational and procedural rules as well."[2] The courts have recognized the breadth of the term, indicating that it encompasses "virtually every statement an agency may make,"[3] including interpretive and substantive rules, guidelines, formal and informal statements, policy proclamations, employee manuals and memoranda of understanding, among other types of actions. Thus a broad range of agency action is potentially subject to congressional review.

The Comptroller General and the Administrator of the Office of Information and Regulatory Affairs (OIRA) of the Office of Management and Budget have particular responsibilities with respect to a "major rule," defined as a rule that will likely have an annual effect on the economy of $100 million or more, increase costs or prices for consumers, industries or state and local governments, or have significant adverse effects on the economy. The determination of whether a rule is major is assigned exclusively to the Administrator of OIRA. Section 804(2). If a rule is deemed major by the OIRA Administrator, the CG must prepare a report for each jurisdictional committee within 15 calendar days of the submission of the agency report required by Section 801 (a)(1) or its publication in the Federal Register, whichever is later.

The statute requires that the CG's report "shall include an assessment of the agency's compliance with the procedural steps required by Section 801(a)(1)(B)."[4] Section 801(a)(2)(A). The CG has interpreted his duty under this provision relatively narrowly as requiring that he determine whether the prescribed action has been taken, i.e., whether a required cost-benefit analysis has been provided, and whether the required actions under the Regulatory Flexibility Act, the Unfunded Mandates Reform Act of 1995, and any other relevant requirements under any other legislation or executive orders were taken, not to examine the substantive adequacy of the actions.

The designation of a rule as major also affects its effective date. A major rule may become effective on the latest of the following scenarios: (1) 60 calendar days after Congress receives the report submitted pursuant to Section 801(a)(1)[5] or after the rule is published in the Federal Register; (2) if Congress passes a joint resolution of disapproval and the President vetoes it, the earlier of when one House votes and fails to override the veto, or 30 calendar days after Congress receives the veto message; or (3) the date the rule would otherwise have taken effect (unless a joint resolution is enacted). Section 801 (a)(3).

Thus the earliest a major rule can become effective is 60 calendar days after the later of the submission of the report required by Section 801 (a)(1) or its publication in the Federal Register, unless some other provision of the law provides an exception for an earlier date. Three possibilities exist. Under Section 808(2) an agency may determine that a rule should become effective notwithstanding Section 801(a)(3) where it finds "good cause that notice and public procedure thereon are impracticable, unnecessary, or contrary to the public interest."[6] Second, the President may determine that a rule should take effect earlier because of an imminent threat to health or safety or other emergency; to insure the enforcement of the criminal laws; for national security purposes; or to implement an international trade agreement. Section 801(c). Finally, a third route is available under Section 801 (a)(5) which provides that "the effective date of a rule shall not be delayed by operation of this chapter beyond the date on which either House of Congress votes to reject a joint resolution of disapproval under Section 802."[7]

All other rules take effect "as otherwise allowed by law" after having been submitted to Congress under Section 801(a)(1). Section 801(a)(4). Under the Administrative Procedure Act, a final rule may go into effect 30 days after it is published in the Federal Register in final form. 5 U.S.C. 553(d). An agency, in its discretion, may delay the effectiveness of a rule for a longer period; or it may put it into effect immediately if good cause is shown.

All covered rules are subject to disapproval even if they have gone into effect. Congress has reserved to itself a review period of at least 60 days. Moreover, if a rule is reported within 60 session days of adjournment of the Senate or 60 legislative days of adjournment of the House, the period during which Congress may consider and pass a joint resolution of disapproval is extended to the next succeeding session of the Congress. Section 801(d)(1). Such held over rules are treated as if they were published on the 15th session day of the Senate and the 15th legislative day of the House in the succeeding session and as though a report under Section 801(a)(1) was submitted on that date. Section 801(d)(2)(A), (e)(2). But a held over rule takes effect as otherwise provided. 801(d)(3). The opportunity for Congress to consider and disapprove is simply extended so that it has a full 60 session or legislative days to act in any session.

If a joint resolution of disapproval is enacted into law, the rule is deemed not to have had any effect at any time. Section 801(f). If a rule that is subject to any statutory, regulatory or judicial deadline for its promulgation is not allowed to take effect, or is terminated by the passage of a joint resolution, any deadline is extended for one year after the date of enactment of the joint resolution. Section 803. A rule that does not take effect, or is not continued because of passage of a disapproval resolution, may not be reissued in substantially the same form. Indeed, before any reissued or new rule that is "substantially the same" as a disapproved rule can be issued it must be specifically authorized by a law enacted subsequent to the disapproval of the original rule. Section 801(b)(2).

Section 802(a) spells out the process for an up or down vote on a joint resolution of disapproval.[8] A joint resolution of disapproval must be introduced within 60 calendar days (excluding days either House of Congress is adjourned for more than three days during a session of Congress) after the agency reports the rule to the Congress in compliance with Section 801 (a)(1). Timely introduction of a disapproval resolution allows each House 60 session or legislative days to consider it through use of expedited consideration procedures, and if passed, allows retroactive nullification of an effective rule, and the limitation on an agency from promulgating a "substantially similar" rule without subsequent congressional authorization to do so by law.

The law provides an expedited consideration procedure for the Senate. If the committee to which a joint resolution is referred has not reported it out within 20 calendar days after referral, it may be discharged from further consideration by a written petition of 30 Members of the Senate, at which point the measure is placed on the calendar. After committee report or discharge it is in order at any time for a motion to proceed to consideration. All points of order against the joint resolution (and against consideration of the measure) are waived, and the motion is not subject to debate, amendment, postponement, or to a motion to proceed to other business. If the motion to consider is agreed to, it remains as unfinished business of the Senate until disposed of. Section 802(d)(1). Debate on the floor is limited to 10 hours. Amendments to the resolution and motions to postpone or to proceed to other business are not in order. Section 802(d)(2). At the conclusion of debate an up or down vote on the joint resolution is to be taken. Section 802(d)(3).[9]

There is no special procedure for expedited consideration and processing of joint resolutions in the House. But if one House passes a joint resolution before the other House acts, the measure of the other House is not referred to a committee. The procedure of the House receiving a joint resolution "shall be the same as if no joint resolution had been received from the other House, but . . . the vote on final passage shall be on the joint resolution of the other House." Section 802(f)(1)(2).

Section 805 precludes judicial review of any "determination, finding, action or omission under this chapter." This would insulate from court review, for example, a determination by the OIRA Administrator that a rule is major or not, a presidential determination that a rule should become effective immediately, an agency determination that "good cause" requires a rule to go into effect at once, or a question as to the adequacy of a Comptroller General's assessment of an agency's report. The legislative history of this provision indicates that this preclusion of judicial review would not apply to a court challenge to a failure of an agency to report a rule. This appears not to be a judicially settled matter.[10]

Finally, the law provides a rule of construction that a reviewing court shall not draw any inference from a congressional failure to enact a joint resolution of disapproval with respect to such rule or a related statute. Section 801(g).

UTILIZATION OF THE REVIEW MECHANISM SINCE 1996

As of March 31, 2008, the Comptroller General had submitted reports pursuant to section 801(a)(2)(A) to Congress on 731 major rules.[11] In addition, GAO had cataloged the submission of 47,540 non-major rules as required by Section 801 (a) (1) (A). To date, 47 joint resolutions of disapproval have been introduced relating to 35 rules. One rule, OSHA's ergonomics standard in March 2001, has been disapproved, an action that some believe to be unique to the circumstances of its passage. Two other rules have been disapproved by the Senate. One, the Federal Communication Commission's 2003 rule relating to broadcast media ownership was disapproved by the Senate during the 108th Congress but was not acted upon by the House. The second, a 2005 Department of Agriculture rule relating to the establishment of minimal risk zones for introduction of bovine spongiform encephalopathy (Mad Cow Disease) was disapproved on March 3, 2005, but its counterpart, H.J.Res. 23, was not acted upon by the House. A third joint resolution, S.J.Res. 20, seeking disapproval of a rule promulgated by the Environmental Protection Agency to delist coal and oil-direct utility units from the new source category list under the Clean Air Act, was defeated in the Senate by a vote of 47-51 on September 13, 2005. The following chart details the subjects and actions taken on the introduced resolutions.

OSHA's ergonomics standard had been controversial since the publication of its initial proposal for rulemaking in 1992 during the Bush Administration. OSHA circulated a draft proposal in 1994 which was met with strong opposition from business interests and the formation of an umbrella organization, the National Coalition on Ergonomics, to oppose its adoption. In 1995 OSHA circulated a modified draft proposal, particularly with respect to coverage and regulatory requirements. At the same time, congressional opposition resulted in appropriations riders that prohibited OSHA from promulgating proposed or final ergonomics regulations during the fiscal years 1995, 1996, and 1998.[12] The riders did not prohibit OSHA from continuing its development work, however, which included questions related to whether scientific knowledge of ergonomics was adequate for rulemaking and whether the cost of implementation of a broad standard would be extraordinarily burdensome to industry. Congress mandated reports from the National Academy of Sciences which found a significant statistical link between workplace exposures and musculoskeletal disorders, but also noted that the exact causative factors and mechanisms are not understood. In 2000, congressional attempts to pass another appropriation rider, as well as stand alone prohibitory legislation, failed, and on November 14, 2000, OSHA issued its final standard which became effective on January 16, 2001.[13] Most employer responsibilities under the new standard, however, were not to begin until October, 2001.

As soon as the rule was issued two industry groups filed suit in the Court of Appeals for the District of Columbia Circuit challenging OSHA's authority to issue the rule, its failure to follow proper procedures, the rationality of its provisions, and the adequacy of its scientific and economics analyses. The intervening 2000 elections also altered the political situation with the election of a President and effective control of both Houses of Congress in the same political party. Opponents of the standard introduced a resolution of disapproval under the CRA, S.J.Res. 16, on March 1, 2001. A discharge petition was filed on March 5, and debate on and passage of the resolution in the Senate occurred on March 6 by a vote of 56-44. That evening the House Rules Committee issued a rule for floor action the next day, and after an hour of debate H.J.Res. 35 was passed on March 7 by a vote of 223-206. The President signed the nullifying measure into law on March 20, 2002.[14]

Table 1. Resolutions of Disapproval Introduced Under the Congressional Review Act (April 1996-October 2007)

Date of Resolution	Number	Sponsor	Agency	Subject	Last Action
104th Congress					
9/17/1996	S.J.Res. 60	Sen. Trent Lott	HCFA/HHS	Hospital reimbursement under Medicare	Failed in passage in Senate by UC
105th Congress					
3/4/1997	H.J.Res. 59	Rep. Don Young (+5)	USFWS/DOI	Polar bear trophies from Canada	Hearing (House Committee on Resources)
3/20/1997	H.J.Res. 67 *(Same as S.J.Res. 25)*	Rep. Roger Wicker (+54)	OSHA/DOL	Occupational exposure to methylene chloride	Referred to Subcommittee of House Committee on Education and the Workforce
4/10/1997	S.J.Res. 25 *(Same as H.J.Res. 67)*	Sen. Thad Cochran (+5)	OSHA/DOL	Occupational exposure to methylene chloride	Referred to Senate Committee on Labor and Human Resources
6/18/1997	H.J.Res. 81	Rep. Joe Scarborough	FCC	Revision of cable television leased commercial access rules	Referred to Subcommittee of House Committee on Commerce
6/10/1998	S.J.Res. 50 *(Same as H.J.Res. 123)*	Sen. Christopher Bond	HCFA/HHS	Surety bond requirements for home health agencies under Medicare and Medicaid programs	Referred to Senate Committee on Finance
6/17/1998	H.J. Res 123 *(Same as S.J.Res. 50)*	Rep. Jim Nussle (+65)	HCFA/HHS	Surety bond requirements for home health agencies under Medicare and Medicaid programs	Referred to Subcommittees of House Committees on Ways and Means and Commerce

Table 1. (Continued).

Date of Resolution	Number	Sponsor	Agency	Subject	Last Action
106th Congress					
5/20/1999	H.J.Res. 55	Rep. Ron Paul (+68)	USPS	Delivery of mail to a commercial mail receiving agency	Referred to Subcommittee of House Committee on Government Reform
7/13/2000	H.J.Res. 104	Rep. Ron Paul	EPA	National pollutant discharge elimination system program and federal antidegradatio n policy and the water quality planning and management regulations concerning total maximum daily load	Referred to Subcommittee of House Committee on Transportation and Infrastructure
7/17/2000	S.J.Res. 50 *(Same as H.J.Res. 106)*	Sen. Michael Crapo (+18)	EPA	Water pollution under the total maximum daily load program	Referred to Senate Committee on Environment and Public Works
7/18/2000	H.J.Res. 105	Rep. Marion Berry (+23)	EPA	Total maximum daily loads under the Federal Water Pollution Control Act	Referred to Subcommittee of House Committee on Transportation and Infrastructure
7/18/2000	H.J.Res. 106 *(Same as S.J.Res. 50)*	Rep. Jay Dickey	EPA	Water pollution under the total maximum daily load program	Referred to Subcommittee of House Committee on Transportation and Infrastructure
107th Congress					

Date of Resolution	Number	Sponsor	Agency	Subject	Last Action
3/1/2001	S.J.Res. 6 *(same as H.J.Res. 35; H.Res. 79 provided for its consideration in the House)*	Sen. Don Nickles (+6)	OSHA/DOL	Ergonomics	Became P.L. 107-5 on 3/20/2001
3/7/2001	H.J.Res. 35 *(same as S.J.Res. 6)*	Rep. Ann Northrup (+32)	OSHA/DOL	Ergonomics	Referred to Subcommittee of House Committee on Education and Workforce
3/15/200 1	H.J.Res. 38	Rep. Ron Paul (+ 14)	HHS	Standards for privacy of individually identifiable health information	Referred to Subcommittees of House Committees on Energy and Commerce, Ways and Means, and Education and the Workforce
3/20/2001	S.J.Res. 9[1]	Sen. Barbara Boxer (+6)	USAID	Restoration of the Mexico City Policy	Referred to Committee on Foreign Relations
4/4/200 1	H.J.Res. 43	Rep. Joe Knollenberg	DOE	Residential central air conditioners and heat pumps	Referred to Subcommittee of House Committee on Energy and Commerce
4/4/200 1	H.J.Res. 44	Rep. Joe Knollenberg	DOE	Clothes washers	Referred to Subcommittee of House Committee on Energy and Commerce
5/22/200 1	S.J.Res. 14	Sen. Barbara Boxer	EPA	Delay in the effective date of new arsenic standard	Referred to Senate Committee on Environment and Public Works

Table 1. (Continued).

Date of Resolution	Number	Sponsor	Agency	Subject	Last Action
5/22/200 1	S.J.Res. 15	Sen. Barbara Boxer	DOE	Postponement of the effective date of energy conservation standards for central air conditioners	Hearing by Senate Committee on Energy and Natural Resources (7/13/2001)
5/14/2002	H.J.Res. 92 *(Same as S.J.Res. 37)*	Rep. Eliot Engel (+56)	HHS	Modification of Medicaid upper payment limit for non-State government owned or operated hospitals	Referred to Subcommittee of House Committee on Energy and Commerce
5/14/2002	S.J.Res. 37 *(Same as H.J.Res. 92)*	Sen. Paul Wellstone (+13)	CMS/HHS	Modification of upper payment limit for non-State government owned or operated hospitals	Referred to Senate Committee on Finance
10/8/2002	S.J.Res. 48 *(Same as H.J.Res. 119)*	Sen. John McCain (+10)	FEC	Prohibited and excessive contributions: non-federal funds or soft money	Referred to Senate Committee on Rules and Administration
10/8/2002	H.J.Res. 119 *(Same as S.J.Res. 48)*	Rep. Christopher Shays (+1)	FEC	Prohibited and excessive contributions: non-federal funds or soft money	Referred to House Committee on House Administration
108th Congress					
1/7/2003	H.J.Res. 3	Rep. William Thomas (+106)	CMS/HHS	Revisions to payment policies under the Medicare physician fee schedule for calendar year 2003 and other items	Referred to House Committees on Energy and Commerce and Ways and Means
3/20/2003	H.J.Res. 41	Rep. Lane Evans	DVA	Acquisition procedures for health-care resources	Referred to House Committees on Veterans Affairs and Government Reform

Date of Resolution	Number	Sponsor	Agency	Subject	Last Action
5/22/2003	H.J.Res. 58	Rep. Thomas Trancredo (+7)	Treasury	Section 3 26(a) of USA PATRIOT ACT (acceptance of certain unverifiable forms of identification by financial institutions)	Referred to Subcommittee of House Committee on Financial Services
7/15/2003	S.J.Res. 17 *(Same as H.J.Res. 72)*	Sen. Byron Dorgan (+24)	FCC	Broadcast media ownership	Passed Senate without amendment by Yea-Nay vote (55-40); not acted on by the House
10/16/2003	H.J.Res. 72 *(Same as S.J.Res. 17)*	Rep. Maurice Hinchey (+2)	FCC	Broadcast media ownership	Referred to Subcommittee of House Committee on Energy and Commerce
4/7/2004	S.J.Res. 31 *(Same as H.R 4236)*	Sen. John Edwards	OCC	Bank activities and regulations	Referred to Senate Committee on Banking, Housing, and Urban Affairs
4/7/2004	S.J.Res. 32 *(Same as H.R 4237)*	Sen. John Edwards	OCC	Bank activities and regulations	Referred to Senate Committee on Banking, Housing, and Urban Affairs
4/28/2004	H.R. 4236 *(Same as S.J.Res. 31)*	Rep. Luis Gutierrez (+35)	OCC	Bank activities and regulations	Referred to Subcommittee of House Committee on Financial Services
4/28/2004	H.R. 4237 *(Same as S.J.Res. 32)*	Rep. Luis Gutierrez (+35)	OCC	Bank activities and regulations	Referred to Subcommittee of House Committee on Financial Services
109th Congress					

Table 1. (Continued).

Date of Resolution	Number	Sponsor	Agency	Subject	Last Action
2/14/2005	S.J.Res. 4 (*Same as H.J.Res. 24)*	Sen. Conrad (+11)	Agriculture	Establishment minimal risk zones for introduction of mad cow disease	Passed Senate by 52-46 Yea-Nay vote 3/3/05; not acted on by House
2/17/2005	H.J.Res. 23 (*Same as S.J.Res. 4*)	Rep. Herseth (+1)	Agriculture	Establishment of minimal risk zones for introduction of mad cow disease	Referred to House Agriculture Committee. No action taken
6/29/2005	S.J.Res. 20 (*Same as H.J.Res. 56*)	Sen. Leahy (+31)	EPA	Removal of coal and oil- fired generating units from list of major sources of hazardous pollutants	Defeated in Senate by 47-51 vote, 9/13/05
6/29/2005	H.J.Res. 56 (*Same as S.J.Res. 20*)	Rep. Meehan (+4)	EPA	Removal of coal and oil- fired generating units from list of major sources of hazardous pollutants	Referred to Committee on Energy and Commerce. No action taken

Date of Resolution	Number	Sponsor	Agency	Subject	Last Action
1 10th Congress					
7/30/2007	H.J.Res. 47	Rep. Zoe Lofgren (+6)	U.S. Citizenship and Immigration Services (DHS)	Adjustment of Immigration and Naturalization Benefit application and petition fee schedule	Referred to House Judiciary Subcommittee on Immigration, no action taken
9/11/2007	S.J.Res. 18 (*Same as H.J. Res 49)*	Sen. Jeff Bingaman (+25)	Centers for Medicare and Medicaid Services (HHS)	Cost limit for providers operated by units of government and other provisions under the Medicaid program	Referred to Senate Finance Committee, no action taken
9/11/2007	H.J.Res. 49 (*Same as S.J.Res. 18*)	Rep. Henry Waxman	Centers for Medicare and Medicaid Services (HHS)	Cost limit for providers by units of government and other provisions under the Medicaid program	Referred to Subcommittee of Health of House Energy and Commerce, no action taken

Table 1. (Continued).

Date of Resolution	Number	Sponsor	Agency	Subject	Last Action
9/24/2007	H.J.Res. 51	Rep. Joe Baca (+13)	U.S. Citizenship and Immigration Services (DHS)	Requiring certain lawful permanent residents to apply for new permanent resident card	Referred to House Judiciary Committee, no action taken.
10/3/2007	H.J.Res. 55 (*Same as S.J.Res. 20)*	Rep. Stephanie Herseth Sandlin (+4)	Agriculture	Relating to importation of cattle and beef.	Referred to House Agriculture Committee, no action taken
10/3/2007	S.J.Res. 20 (*Same as H.J.Res. 55)*	Sen. Byron L. Dorgan (+9)	Agriculture	Relating to importation of cattle and beef.	Referred to Senate Agriculture Committee, no action taken
10/22/2007	S.J.Res. 22	Sen. Max Baucus (+30)	Centers for Medicare and Medicaid Services (HHS)	Medicare coverage for the use of erythropoiesis stimulating agents in cancer and related neoplastic conditions	Referred to Senate Finance Committee.

Date of Resolution	Number	Sponsor	Agency	Subject	Last Action
3/5/2008	S.J.Res. 28 (*Same as H.J.Res. 79)*	Sen. Byron Dorgan (+27)	Federal Communica-tions Commission	Broadcast media ownership	Sen. Committee on Commerce, Science, and Transportation ordered the joint resolution to be reported favorably without amendment on 4/24/08.
3/13/2008	H.J.Res. 79 (*Same as S.J.Res. 28*)	Rep. Jay Inslee (+8)	Federal Communica tions Commission	Broadcast media ownership	Referred to H. Energy and Commerce Committee, Subcommittee on Telecommunicatio n and the Internet.
3/13/2008	H.J.Res. 78 (*Same as S.J.Res. 30*)	Rep. Keith Ellison (+6)	Centers for Medicare and Medicaid (HHS)	State plan case management under Medicaid Program	Referred to House Energy and Commerce Committee, Subcommittee on Health.
3/13/2008	S.J.Res. 30 (*Same as H.J.Res 78*)	Sen. Barbara Mikulski (+18)	Centers for Medicare and Medicaid (HHS)	State plan case management under Medicaid Program	Referred to Senate Finance Committee.

Note: Not included in this tabulation are bills designed to disapprove agency rules but that were not joint resolutions under the Congressional Review Act. For example, H.R. 3735, introduced on April 28, 1998, by Rep. Ron Paul, was intended to disapprove a rule requiring the use of bycatch reduction devices in the shrimp fishery of the Gulf of Mexico. The bill was in response to Amendment 9 to the Fishery Management Plan for the Shrimp Fishery of the Gulf of Mexico, issued as a final rule implementing the amendment on April 14, 1998. The bill's findings section indicated that approval of the amendment was inconsistent with the requirements of the Magnuson-Stevens Fishery Conservation Act and the Administrative Procedure Act. The disapproval section indicated that the rule "shall have no force or effect."

1. On June 22, 2001, Senator Boxer also introduced S.J.Res. 17, which was intended to disapprove a memorandum issued by the President on March 29, 2001, (66 FR 17301) restoring the Mexico City Policy. However, the Congressional Review Act does not apply to actions by the President. See text at pp. 16-17.

In sum, the veto of the ergonomics standards could be seen as the product of an unusual, confluence of factors and events: control of both Houses of Congress and the presidency by the same party, the longstanding opposition by these political actors, as well as by broad components of the industry to be regulated, to the ergonomics standards, and the willingness and encouragement of a President seeking to undo a contentious, end-of-term rule from a previous Administration.

In all other cases, if there is any discernible pattern to the introduced resolutions, it is to exert pressure on the subject agencies to modify or withdraw the rule, or to elicit support of Members, which in some instances was successful. For example, H.J.Res. 67 (1997) was aimed at disapproving an Occupational Health and Safety Administration (OSHA) rule setting occupational exposure limits on methylene chloride, a paint stripper used in the furniture and airplane industries. Its sponsor, Representative Roger Wicker, contended that the rule would harm small businesses without increasing protections for workers. The disapproval resolution never received a floor vote. But the Congressman succeeded in effecting a compromise through the inclusion of provisions in the FY1998 Labor, HHS and Education appropriations measure[15] which required OSHA to provide on-site assistance for companies to comply with the new rules without fear of penalty. Mr. Wicker is reported to have stated that he used the disapproval resolution as a vehicle to gather support from influential Members, including the chairs of the House Appropriations and Commerce Committees.[16]

The disapproval resolution mechanism was effectively utilized to accomplish the suspension of a highly controversial rulemaking by the then-Health Care Financing Administration (HCFA). In January 1998, HCFA issued a rule requiring that home health agencies (HHAs) participating in the Medicare program must obtain a surety bond that is the greater of $50,000 or 15 percent of the annual amount paid to the HHA by the Medicare program. In addition, a new HHA entering the Medicare or Medicaid program after January 1, 1998, had to meet a capitalization requirement by showing it actually had available sufficient capital to start and operate the HHA for the first three months. The rule was issued without the usual public participation through notice and comment and was made immediately effective. Substantial opposition to the rule quickly surfaced from both surety and HHA industry representatives. HCFA attempted to remedy the complaints by twice amending the rule, in March and in June, but was unsuccessful in quelling the industry concerns. On June 10, Senator Bond, for himself and 13 other co-sponsors, introduced S.J.Res. 50 to disapprove the June 1 HCFA rule. Within a short period, the disapproval resolution had garnered 52 sponsors. On June 17, a companion bill, H.J.Res. 123, was introduced in the House. Thereafter, according to press reports, members of the staffs of Senators Bond, Baucus, and Grassley (all members of the

Senate Finance Committee with jurisdiction over the agency) met with HCFA officials and concluded an agreement that (1) the agency would suspend its June 1, 1998 rule indefinitely; (2) a General Accounting Office report would be requested by the committee that would study the issues surrounding the surety bond requirement; (3) on completion and issuance of the GAO report, HCFA would work in consultation with the Congress about the surety bond requirement; and (4) any new rule would not be effective earlier than February 15, 1999, and would be preceded by at least 60 days prior notice. The agreement reportedly was memorialized in a June 26 letter to HCFA signed by Senators Bond, Baucus and Grassley.[17] The GAO report was issued on January 29, 1999, but the rule suspension was never lifted. No floor vote on the disapproval resolutions occurred in either House.

Another illustration of the manner in which the review mechanism has been utilized is shown by S.J.Res. 60 (1996), concerning another HCFA rule, this one dealing with the agency's annual revision of the rates for reimbursement of Medicare providers (doctors and hospitals), which normally would have been effective on October 1, 1996. HCFA, however, submitted the rule to Congress on August 30, 1996, and since it was a major rule, it could not go into effect for 60 days, or until October 29, which meant there would be a significant loss of revenues because the differential rate increases could not be imposed for most of the month of October. Section 801(a)(5), however, provides that if a joint resolution of disapproval is rejected by one House, "the effective date of a rule shall not be delayed by operation of this chapter..." On the morning of September 17, 1996, Senator Lott introduced S.J.Res. 60 and that afternoon, by unanimous consent, the resolution "was deemed not passed."[18] The HCFA rule went into effect on October 1 as scheduled.

A final interesting utilization of the CRA process that had an impact and resulted in an unusual outcome, involved President George W. Bush's restoration, on February 15, 2001, of President Reagan's so-called Mexico City Policy, which limited the use of federal and non-federal monies by non-governmental organizations (NGOs) to directly fund foreign population planning programs which support abortion or abortion-related activities. President Clinton had rescinded the 1984 Reagan policy when he took office in January 1993.[19] A President's authority to determine the terms and conditions on which such NGOs may engage in foreign population planning programs derives from the Foreign Assistance Act of 1961.[20] The provision vests the authority to make these determinations exclusively in the Chief Executive. President Reagan delegated his authority to make the determinations to the Administrator of the U.S. Agency for International Development (AID), who issued regulations that specified the conditions upon which grants would be given to NGOs. Thus, when the Mexico City Policy was rescinded in 1993, it was the AID Administrator that did it, at the direction of President Clinton. When President Bush restored it in 2001, he did it in a directive to the AID Administrator[21] who simply revived the old conditions by internal agency administrative action.

A number of Senate opponents of the policy filed a disapproval resolution on March 20, 2001, S.J.Res. 9, to nullify the Administrator's action, reasoning that it was a covered rule under the CRA since the implementing action was taken by an executive agency official and not by the President himself, and thus was reviewable by Congress.[22] The President responded by rescinding his earlier directive to the AID Administrator and thereafter issuing an executive directive under his statutory authority implementing the necessary conditions and limitations for NGO grants.[23] The presidential action mooted the disapproval resolution, and rendered a subsequent attempt to veto by S.J.Res. 17 ineffective because the CRA does not reach such actions by the President.

DISCUSSION

In the 11-plus years since its passage, the CRA process has been used sparingly. Several criticisms and questions concerning the process have been raised by those supporting the wider use of the regulatory disapproving mechanism. These have included a need for a screening mechanism for submitted rules; the absence of an expedited procedure in the House of Representatives for consideration of disapproval resolutions;the deterrent effect of the need for a supermajority to overcome a veto; the scope of the law's coverage; the judicial enforceability of its key requirements; whether a disapproval resolution may be directed at part of a rule; and the effect of a rule nullification on future agency rulemaking in the same area, which, critics believe, have introduced uncertainties and impediments to concerning the use of the process.

1. Lack of a Screening Mechanism to Pinpoint Rules that Need Congressional Review; Proposals for Change

Proponents of an expanded use of the CRA process have called for a screening mechanism that would alert committees to rules that may raise important or sensitive substantive issues. In this view, the perceived lack of timely substantive information prevents busy committees from prioritizing such issues. The Comptroller General's reports on major rules serve as check lists as to whether legally required agency tasks have been done and not as substantive assessments of whether they were done properly or whether the rules accord with congressional intent.

Lack of knowledge of the *existence* of such sensitive rules by jurisdictional committees or interested Members is rarely the case. What critics say is absent is in-depth scrutiny and analysis of individual rules by an authoritative and presumably neutral source that may provide the basis for triggering meaningful congressional review. Opponents reject this argument and often conclude that the act, in its current form, is exactly what Congress intended, and that lack of action under it does not equate to lack of knowledge of major rules.

Some support for an independent substantive screening body was signaled by the introduction by Representative Sue Kelly of H.R. 1704 in the 105th Congress, a bill that would have established a Congressional Office of Regulatory Analysis.[24] The bill was referred to the House Judiciary and Governmental Reform and Oversight Committees both of which favorably reported differing versions of the legislation.[25] Both versions would have established an independent Congressional Office of Regulatory Analysis (CORA) to be headed by a director appointed by the House Speaker and the Senate Majority Leader for a term of four years, with service in the office limited to no more than three terms. The current review functions of the Comptroller General under the CRA and the Congressional Budget Office under the Unfunded Mandates Act of 1995 would have been transferred to the proposed CORA. The Judiciary Committee's version, in addition to having the Office make "an assessment of an agency's compliance with the procedural steps for 'major rules'" required by CRA, directs the proposed CORA to "conduct its own regulatory impact of these 'major rules.'"[26] The bill as reported by the Government Reform Committee would have allowed the CORA director to use "any data and analyses generated by the Federal agency and any data of the Office" in analyzing the submitted rule. Both bills provided that a similar analysis of non-major rules was to be conducted when requested to do so by a House or Senate Committee or by individual Members of either House. First priority for the conduct of such analyses was given to all major rules. Secondary priority was assigned to committee requests. Tertiary priority was given individual Member requests. Finally, under the Judiciary Committee version, the report was to be furnished within 45 days after Congress received notification of the rule; the Governmental Reform bill would have allowed 30 days. H.R. 1704 received no floor action during the 105th Congress.

Critics argue that an independent office of regulatory analysis would serve the congressional need for objective information necessary to evaluate agency regulations. In their view, it would also provide credibility and impetus for wider utilization of the review mechanism. Further, by providing intensive review of certain non-major rules, the possibility of OIRA "hiding" significant rules by not designating them as "major" is forestalled. Those opposing the establishment of an office of this kind would argue that creation of a new congressional bureaucracy for review purposes would be unnecessarily duplicative of what the agencies have already done as well as extraordinarily expensive. The requirement of the Judiciary Committee's version that a CORA do its own cost-benefit analysis from scratch could be pointed to as an unknown cost factor, as well as a task that may not be possible to perform adequately within the allotted 45 days.

Congress agreed upon a limited test of the CORA concept, late in the 106th Congress, with the passage of the Truth in Regulating Act of 2000.[27] That legislation established a three year pilot project for the General Accounting Office (now renamed the Government Accountability Office (GAO)) to report to Congress on economically significant rules. Under this pilot program, whenever an agency published an economically significant proposed or final rule a chairman or ranking minority member of a committee of jurisdiction of either House of Congress may request the Comptroller General (CG) to review the rule. The CG was to report on each rule within 180 calendar days. The report had to contain an "independent evaluation" by the CG of the agency's cost-benefit analysis. We are aware of only one request ever made pursuant to the provision. That was submitted in January 2001 by the chairs of the jurisdictional committees of the House and Senate with respect to the Department of Agriculture's forest planning and roadless area rule. GAO advised the requesters that although Act authorized $5.2 million per year for the program, no monies had been appropriated and it could not proceed with the request. No further action was taken on the request and Congress never enacted an appropriation, thereby forestalling implementation of the project. It may be noted that the 180-day reporting period did not mesh exactly with the time period under the CRA for consideration of rules subject to resolution of disapproval, although completed requests for analyses of *proposed* rules might coincide with such reviews. In any event, the pilot program established by the act expired in January 2004.

In the 109th Congress, Representative Sue Kelly introduced H.R. 1167, which would have made permanent the authority of Congress to request GAO to perform regulatory analyses. The proposed new Truth in Regulating Act (TIRA), if enacted as a permanent responsibility of the GAO, did not appear to provide a specific appropriation to require agency performance of the vested task as was the case when it was previously established as a "pilot project." The act would have, in effect, established an unfunded mandate. Although GAO currently does (and historically has always done) some reviews of agencies' rules at Members' requests under its current appropriations, both the volume and nature of the reviews under this proposal would likely have been substantially different and might have affected its ability to conduct other agency reviews. A similar bill, H.R. 725, section 5, would also have made TIRA permanent, but would have authorized up to $5 million for the reviews.

In an apparent attempt to avoid the criticisms of the CORA model and to remedy some of the perceived impediments to the effectiveness of the CRA, Representative Ginny Brown-Waite introduced H.R. 3356, the Joint Administrative Procedures Committee Act of 2003, in the 108th Congress which would have amended the CRA by establishing a joint congressional committee with broad authority to investigate, evaluate and recommend actions with respect to the development of proposed rules, the amendment or repeal of existing rules, and disapproval of final rules submitted for review under the CRA.[28] The responsibilities would have been in addition to the current statutory framework providing for review of new rules that are required to be reported. A new provision would permit the joint committee to recommend disapproval of new rules to jurisdictional committees. The Judiciary Committee referred it to its Subcommittee on Commercial and Administrative Law. No action was taken by either Committee. Representative Brown-Waite's proposal was reintroduced in the 109th Congress as H.R. 3148 but received no action.

Another bill, H.R. 576, introduced by Representative Ney in the 1 09th Congress, was similar in many respects to H.R. 3148, but quite different in certain fundamental ways. Both would have created a 24 member House-Senate joint committee capable of holding hearings, requiring the attendance of witnesses, and making rules regarding its organization and procedures. Both also provided for an expedited consideration procedure in the House. Significant differences appear, however, with respect to the roles assigned to the joint committees. Under H.R. 3148, the current process established by the CRA for congressional review of new agency rules would have been maintained: required reports on new rulemakings would be submitted to each House and such reports sent to the jurisdictional committees of each House for action. Rules required to be reported would also be sent to the joint committee. Special rules were provided for discharge from committees in the Senate and, under proposed H.R. 3148, from House committees. Expedited procedures are in effect for floor proceedings in each House. The only part to be played by the joint committee in this rule review process under H.R. 3148 would have been to recommend to jurisdictional committees that certain submitted new rules be subject to disapproval resolutions. Deference to the current roles of jurisdictional committees was also maintained under H.R. 3148 with respect to the new duties given to the joint committee to selectively review existing federal agency rules in effect before the enactment of the CRA and existing major rules of federal agencies promulgated since April 1996.

Under H.R. 576, the joint committee, rather than the jurisdictional committees of each House, would have received the report of covered rules submitted for review by federal agencies as well as cost-benefit analyses and other materials. Jurisdictional committees would receive copies of these materials from the joint committee. GAO was to submit its report on major rules to the joint committee, not the jurisdictional committees concerned. Major rules could have taken effect no earlier than 60 days after the rule was published in the *Federal Register* or is received by the joint committee. Joint resolutions of disapproval ere to be reported by the joint committee to the respective Houses for action. The joint committee could also report "by bill ... recommendations with respect to matters within the jurisdiction of their respective Houses which are referred to the joint committee or otherwise within the jurisdiction of the joint committee." It would appear, then, that the joint committee would have had the predominant role in the congressional review process, which might inject a highly controversial issue - - diminution of the role of jurisdictional committees.

A third bill introduced in the 1 09th Congress was H.R. 931, by Representative Hayworth, which would have prohibited any regulation proposed by a federal agency from going into effect until a bill enacted under expedited consideration procedures applicable to to the rule was signed into law. The term "regulation" was given the broad meaning of the term "rule" as defined in 5 U.S.C. 55 1(4). The bill did not specifically reference the current CRA process. In fact, it would have superceded it and required rulemaking agencies to seek approval of all covered "regulations." There was no provision for congressional processing in a timely and expeditious manner a potentially huge member proposed regulations.

2. Lack of an Expedited House Procedure

Those unsatisfied with the current procedure argue that the current absence of an expedited consideration procedure in the House of Representatives may well be a factor affecting use of the process in that body since, as a practical matter, it will mean engaging the House leadership each time a rule is deemed important enough by a committee or group of Members to seek speedy access to the floor. In view of the limits both on floor time and the ability to gain the attention of the leadership, it is argued that only the most well situated in the body will be able to gain access within the limited period of review.[29] It is also maintained that a perception that no action will be taken in the House might deter Senate action.

3. The Deterrent Effect of the Ultimate Need for a Supermajority to Veto a Rule

A consideration that critics maintain limits expanded use of the full CRA review mechanism has been the realization that any joint resolution disapproving a rule that does not have the support of the Administration would be vetoed and require a two-thirds vote in each House to override. The deterrent potential of the need for a supermajority in each House to overcome a presidential veto is likely to be significant, unless the object of the exercise is simply to provide the impetus for informal accommodations, such as occurred in the HCFA surety bond matter, or to influence Members to support alternative legislation. Critics assert that a realization by agencies over time that passage of a disapproval resolution is highly unlikely could substantially reduce the efficacy of such a threat. Additionally, they maintain that a possible consequence of such an assumption is that agencies will not factor in congressional disapproval as part of the rule development process.[30]. Since the ergonomics veto, 19 resolutions of disapproval with respect to 14 rules have been introduced, only one of which has been acted upon (by one House),[31] which some see as a return to the prior practice of using the mechanism to facilitate bargaining.

Thus, even with the disapproval of the ergonomics standard, critics are concerned about the possible effect of the supermajority requirement. Some have proposed a multi-tiered disapproval mechanism. That is, instead of all rules, major or non-major, being treated equally in that they can only be overturned by a joint resolution of disapproval, some rules might be designated for more selective, special review. For example, some argue that major or significant rules might be subject to a joint resolution of *approval*. Under such a scheme a major or significant rule would not become effective unless a joint resolution approving it passed both Houses within a specified period of time.[32] To make such a scheme effective someone or some body, would need the authority to designate which rules are “major” or “significant” and thereby subject to the affirmative approval requirement. The burden for supporting and justifying such rules would fall on the promulgating agencies. All other rules would be subject to disapproval resolutions. Another proposal is to subject all covered rules to congressional approval and establish an expedited procedure whereby non-controversial rules may be sped through leaving only a few for close consideration.[33]

4. The Reluctance to Disapprove an Omnibus Rule where Only One Part of the Rule Raises Objection

Section 808 of the review provision sets forth the mandatory text of any joint resolution of disapproval: "That Congress disapproves the rule submitted by the relating , and such rule shall have no force or effect. (The blank spaces being appropriately filled in)." The quoted text refers to "the rule" and "such rule," indicating a rule in its entirety. The experience of 33 joint resolutions of disapproval thus far introduced is that the first blank is filled with the name of the promulgating agency and the second with a generic title or description of the rule.[34] Similarly, the text of the review provision refers to "such rule," "a rule," or "the rule," with no language expressly referring to a part of any rule under review. The procedure leading to a vote on the proposed disapproval resolution allows for no amendments, and the final vote is up or down on the joint resolution as introduced.

The legislative history of the provision is similarly uniform in using language that would ordinarily indicate a reference to a submitted rule in its entirety, except in one instance. During a discussion of the Section 802 procedure that would obtain when one House completes its action on a joint resolution and sends to it to the other House before the second House has yet to complete any action, the following comment is made:

> . . .Subsection 802(f) sets forth one unique provision that does not expire in either House. Subsection 802(f) provides procedures for passage of a joint resolution of disapproval when one House passes a joint resolution and transmits it to the other House that has not yet completed action. In both Houses, the joint resolution of the first House to act shall not be referred to a committee but shall be held at the desk. In the Senate, a House-passed resolution may be considered directly only under normal Senate procedures, regardless of when it is received by the Senate. A resolution of disapproval that originated in the Senate may be considered under the expedited procedures only during the period specified in subsection 802(e). Regardless of the procedures used to consider a joint resolution in either House, the final vote of the second House shall be on the joint resolution of the first House (no matter when that vote takes place). *If the second House passes the resolution, no conference is necessary and the joint resolution will be presented to the President for his signature. Subsection 802(f) is justified because subsection 802(a) sets forth the required language of a joint resolution in each House, and thus, permits little variance in the joint resolutions that could be introduced in each House.[35]* (Emphasis supplied).

The last two sentences are seen by some as raising uncertainty. The next to last sentence would appear to contemplate the possibility of a conference to resolve differences in resolutions. The last sentence minimizes what those differences could be. Some have suggested that the explanation contemplates that parts of rules may be the subject of disapproval resolutions, arguing that the framers of the provision would have known that many rules are complex and contain a variety of provisions, only one or a few of which may be objectionable, and would not have required a whole rulemaking to be brought down simply because of one offending portion out of many. It has also been argued that in light of the Section 801(b)(2) prohibition against agency issuance of a rule "in substantially the same form" after passage of a disapproval resolution unless Congress by subsequent law authorizes it, not allowing rejection of part of a rule would have a draconian result.

An up or down vote on the entire rule would appear to have been the intent of the framers of the review provision. The language and structure of the provision, and the supporting explanation of the legislative history, contemplates a speedy, definitive and limited process. It is not unlike the legislative processes created for congressional actions dealing with military base closings,[36] international trade agreements,[37] and presidential reorganization plans,[38] among others. Each dealt with complex, politically sensitive decisions which allowed only an up or down vote by the Congress on the entire package presented. It was understood that piecemeal consideration would delay and perhaps obstruct legislative resolution of the issues before it. For similar reasons, the statutory structure and legislative history of the review provision strongly indicate that Congress intended the process to focus on submitted rules as a whole and not to allow veto of individual parts. Perhaps a proper reading of the quoted portion of the legislative history is that it was contemplating the possibility that the blank to be filled in after "relating to" might have different generic descriptions of the rule subject to disapproval. A broader reading of these sentences would not otherwise appear warranted by either the legislative language itself or the rest of the explanatory legislative history.

As a practical matter, if this reading is correct it may be a factor in the limited use of the mechanism. As indicated, nullifying a rule means disabling an agency from regulating in the area covered by the rule unless Congress passes further authorization legislation, a significant consequence of any disapproval action. On the other hand, expressly authorizing nullification of portions of a rule might allow competing disapproval resolutions within each House and the certainty of a long, drawn out conference with the possibility of no agreement.

5. The Uncertainty of which Rules Are Covered by the CRA

The drafers of the congressional review provision arguably adopted the broadest possible definition of the term "rule" when they incorporated Section 551(4) of the APA. As indicated previously,[39] the legislative history of Section 551(4) and the case law interpreting it make clear that it was meant to encompass all substantive rulemaking documents — these may include policy statements, guidances, manuals, circulars, memoranda, bulletins and the like — which as a legal or practical matter an agency wishes to make binding on the affected public.

The legislative history of the CRA emphasizes that by adoption of the Section 551 (4) definition of rule, the review process would not be limited only to coverage of rules required to comply with the notice and comment provisions of the APA or any other statutorily required variations of notice and comment procedures, but would rather encompass a wider spectrum of agency activities characterized by their effect on the regulated public: "The committee's intent in these subsections is . . . to include matters that substantially affect the rights or obligations of outside parties. The essential focus of this inquiry is not on the type of rule but on its effect on the rights and obligations of non-agency parties."[40] The drafters of the legislation indicated their awareness of the practice of agencies avoiding the notification and public participation requirements of APA notice-and-comment rulemaking by utilizing the issuance of other documents as a means of binding the public, either legally or practically,[41] and noted that it was the intent of the legislation to subject just such documents to congressional scrutiny:

> . . . The committees are concerned that some agencies have attempted to circumvent notice-and-comment requirements by trying to give legal effect to general statements of policy, "guidelines," and agency policy and procedure manuals. The committees admonish the agencies that the APA's broad definition of "rule" was adopted by the authors of this legislation to discourage circumvention of the requirements of chapter 8.[42]

It is likely that virtually all the 45,433 non-major rules thus far reported to the Comptroller General have been either notice and comment rules or agency documents required to be published in the Federal Register. The legislation's sponsors indicated that perhaps thousands of covered rules have not been submitted for review.[43] Defining an exact number is difficult since such covered documents are rarely published in the Federal Register and thus may come to the attention of committees or Members serendipitously or through complaints of interest groups.

Nine agency actions came to the attention of committee chairmen and Members and were referred to the Comptroller General for determinations whether they were covered rules. In six of the nine cases the CG determined the action documents to be covered rules. For example, in a letter to the Honorable John D. Rockefeller, IV, Chairman, Senate Subcommittee on Health Care, Committee on Finance, and the Honorable Olympia Snowe, Ranking Minority Member, Senate Subcommittee on Health Care, Committee on Finance, B-3 16048 April 17, 2008 the GAO General Counsel stated that an August 17, 2007 letter issued by the Centers for Medicare and Medicaid Services (CMS) to state officials concerning the State Children's Health Insurance Program (SCHIP) was "a rule that must be submitted for review under the CRA before it can take effect because it is a statement of general applicability and future effect designed to implement, interpret, or prescribe law or policy with regard to the SCHIP program." See also, a letter to Honorable Lane Evans, Ranking Minority Member, House Committee on Veterans' Affairs, B-292045 (May 19, 2003) (Department of Veterans Affairs memorandum terminating the Department's Vendee Loan Program is not a rule that must be submitted to Congress because it is exempt under Section 804(3)(B) and (C) as a rule relating to "agency management" or "agency organization, procedure, or practice that does not substantially affect the rights or obligations of non-agency parties."); letter to Honorable Ted Strickland, B29 1906 (February 28, 2003) (Department of Veterans Affairs memorandum instructing all directors of health care networks to cease any marketing activities to enroll new veterans in such networks is excluded from CRA coverage by Section 804(3)(C) which excludes "any agency rule of agency organization, procedure, or practice that does not substantially affect the rights or obligations of non-agency parties."); letter to Honorable Doug Ose, Chairman, House Subcommittee on Energy Policy, Natural Resources, and Regulatory Affairs, Committee on Government Reform, B-287557 (May 14, 2001)(Department of Interior's Fish and Wildlife Service's Trinity River "Record of Decision" is a rule covered by the CRA because it is an agency statement of general applicability and future effect designed to implement, interpret, or prescribe law or policy and is an "agency action[] that substantially affect[s] the rights and obligations of outside parties."); letter to the Honorable James A. Leach, Chairman, House Banking Committee, B-286338 (October 17, 2000)(Farm Credit Administration's national charter initiative held to be a rule under the CRA); letter to Honorable David M. McIntosh, Chairman, Subcommittee on National Economic Growth, Natural Resources, and Regulatory Affairs, House Committee on Government Reform and Oversight, B-281575 (January 20, 1999) (EPA "Interim Guidance for Investigating Title VI Administrative Complaints Challenging Permits" held to be covered because it created new, mandatory steps in the procedure for handling disparate impact assessments which gave recipients new rights they did not previously possess for obtaining complaint dismissals, a substantive alteration of the previous regulation.); letter to Honorable Conrad Burns, B-278224 (November 10, 1997) (the American Heritage River Initiative announced by the Council on Environmental Quality was not a covered rule because it was established by presidential executive order and direction and the President is not an "agency" under the APA and is not subject to the provisions of the APA); letter to Honorable Ted Stevens, Chairman, Senate Appropriations Committee, et al, B-275 178 (July 3, 1997) (Tongass National Forest Land and Resources Management Plan held an agency statement of general applicability and future effect that implements, interprets, and prescribes law and policy); letter to Honorable Larry Craig, Chairman, Senate Committee on Energy and Resources, B-274505 (September 16, 1996) (memorandum of Secretary of Agriculture concerning the Emergency Salvage Timber Sale Program held to be a covered rule because it is of general applicability and interprets and implements the statutory program).

The GAO opinion on the American Heritage River Initiative rests its rationale that a presidential directive to an agency that results in substantive action by that agency is not thereby covered by the CRA based on the Supreme Court's rulings in *Franklin* v. *Massachusetts*, 505 U.S. 788, 800 (1992) and *Dalton* v. *Spector*, 511 U.S. 462, 469 (1994). In light of *Chamber of Commerce* v. *Reich*, 74 F. 3d 1322 (D.C. Cir. 1996) and *National Family Planning* v. *Sullivan*, 979 F. 2d 227 (1992), which successfully challenged substantive changes in rules that were directed by a presidential directive, the GAO General Counsel's conclusions may be questioned.

Also, the General Counsel's analysis in its February 28, 2003 opinion concluding that a Department of Veterans Affairs (DVA) memo terminating a long-time veterans health outreach program was an exempt agency practice that had no substantial effect on the rights of non-agency parties may be questioned. In contrast with its May 19, 2004, opinion dealing with a termination of a DVA vendee loan program, where it closely examined the statutory basis of the loan program and found that it was established on the basis of *discretionary* authority of the Secretary and provided no direct benefits to veterans, the General Counsel made no mention that the Congress had charged the Secretary of DVA "with the affirmative duty of seeking out eligible veterans and eligible dependants and providing them" with federal benefits and services. Representative Strickland joined with the Vietnam Veterans of American in a suit seeking declaratory and injunctive relief to restore the program. In *Vietnam Veterans of America v. Principi*, 2005 WL 901133 (D.D.C. March 11, 2005), the district court found that "[u]nder 38 U.S.C. 7721, 7722, and 7227, Congress charges the Secretary of the Department of Veterans Affairs with the affirmative duty to 'provide outreach services.' This duty is not discretionary but must be done in accordance with Congress' wishes." The court concluded, however, that since Congress appropriated a lump-sum for both outreach services and health care services, and the record showed that some monies had been expended for outreach services, Congress meant to allow the Secretary the discretion to decide "the manner in which [outreach services] are to be provided." The critique here is that the Comptroller General's failure to examine the Secretary's duty under the statute in question eliminated the possibility finding a substantial effect of the agency's action on the rights or obligations of non-agency parties. It is interesting to note that subsequent to the CG's decision and the filing of the lawsuit, Congress enacted a limitation on the Fiscal Year 2004 VA appropriation stating, '[n]one of the funds made available may be used to implement any policy prohibiting the Directors of the Veterans Integrated Service Networks from conducting outreach or marketing to enroll new veterans within their respective networks," a possible indication that Congress thought the controverted policy could be having an impact on potential beneficiaries. See P.L. 108-199, H.R. 2673, sec. 418 (2004).

Believing such instances to be only a small portion of unreported agency actions, GAO, at the behest of the House Government Reform and Oversight Subcommittee on National Economic Growth, Natural Resources, and Regulatory Affairs, engaged in discussions with the Office of Management (OMB) during 1998 for the creation of a uniform reporting form for use by agencies in reporting covered rules to the CG, and for the promulgation of an OMB guidance document covering such matters under the review provision as the definition of a covered rule, reporting requirements, the good cause exemption, and the consequences of failing to report a rule, among others. The failure to issue such guidance prompted insertion of the following directive in the FY1 999 appropriation for OMB: "OMB is directed to submit a report by March 31, 1999, to the Committees on Appropriations, the Senate Committee on Governmental Affairs, and the House Committee on Government Reform and Oversight that . . . issues guidance on the requirements of 5 U.S.C. Sec. 801 (a) (1) and (3); sections 804 (3), and 808 (2), including a standard new rule reporting form for use under section 801 (a)(1)(A)-(B)."[44] OMB in the view of the Subcommittee, "has failed to to substantially comply with that statutory directive."[45]

6. The Uncertainty of the Effect of an Agency's Failure to Report a Covered Rule to Congress

Section 801(a)(1)(A) of the CRA provides that "[b]efore a rule can take effect," the Federal agency promulgating such rule shall submit to each House of Congress and the Comptroller General a report containing the text of the rule, a description of the rule, including whether it is a major rule, and its proposed effective date. Section 805 states that "no determination, finding, action or omission under this chapter shall be subject to judicial review." The Department of Justice (DOJ) has broadly hinted that the language of Section 805 "precluding judicial review is unusually sweeping" so that it would presumably prevent judicial scrutiny and sanction of an agency's failure to report a covered rule.[46] DOJ has succeeded with its preclusion argument in two federal district court rulings. Later the rationale of those opinions was called into question and rejected by a third district court.

In *Texas Savings and Community Bankers Assoc. v. Federal Housing Finance Board*,[47] three thrift associations and two of their trade associations sued the Federal Housing Finance Board challenging one of its policies regarding the home mortgage lending industry. The plaintiff's argued, *inter alia*, that the policy was a rule required to be reported to Congress under the CRA and the failure to report it precluded its enforcement. The government argued that Section 805 was a blanket preclusion of judicial review. In response to plaintiff's contention that Section 805 only precluded review of any "determination, finding, or omission" by Congress, the court held that "the statute provides for no judicial review of any 'any determination, finding, action or omission under this chapter,' not 'by Congress under this chapter.' The court must follow the plain English. Apparently, Congress seeks to enforce the [CRA] without the able assistance of the courts."[48] The court made no reference to the scheme of the act or its legislative history.

The Texas district court's "plain meaning" rationale was cited with approval by an Ohio district in *United States v. American Electric Power Service Corp.*[49] That case was one of many involving extensive litigation by the Environmental Protection Agency (EPA), begun in the mid-1990's to establish the extent to which a power plant or factory may alter its facilities or operations without bringing about a "modification" of that emission source so as to trigger the Clean Air Act's New Source Performance Standards and pre-construction "new source review."[50] Among the issues common in these cases, and raised in this case, was whether EPA's determination to initiate litigation enforcement after many years of no enforcement was a substantive change that had to be reported to Congress under the CRA. It was among 123 affirmative defenses raised by defendants, nine coal-fired power plants in Ohio, Virginia, and West Virginia, which the Government moved to dismiss. Citing the *Texas Savings* case approvingly, the district court agreed "that the language of Section 805 is plain" and that "[d]eparture from the plain language is appropriate in the 'rare cases [in which] the literal application of a statute would produce a result demonstrably at odds with the intention of its drafters ... or when the statutory language is ambiguous.'... In all other cases, the plain meaning of the statute controls."[51] The court did not indicate whether it had attempted to discern whether there was any evidence of congressional intent at odds with the court's plain meaning reading. It did, however, provide an alternative rationale: "Furthermore, this Court is not convinced that the instant enforcement action amounts to rulemaking which would be covered by 5 U.S.C. 801 *et. seq*., in the first instance," without elaboration.[52]

In *United States v. Southern Indiana Gas and Electric Co*.,[53] the court faced the same issue in a motion for summary judgment by the power company defendant. Rejecting the *Texas Savings* and *American Electric Power* precedents, it found that Section 805 is ambiguous and susceptible to two possible meanings: that Congress did not intend for any court review of an agency's compliance with the CRA or that Congress only intended to preclude judicial review of its own determination, findings, actions or omissions made under the CRA *after* a rule had been submitted to it for review. Adopting the first alternative, argued for by the Government and adopted by the *Texas Savings* and *American Electric Power* courts, would, according to the court, allow agencies "to evade the strictures of the CRA by simply not reporting new rules and courts would be barred from reviewing their lack of compliance. This result would be at odds with the purpose of the CRA, which is to provide a check on administrative agencies' power to set policies and essentially legislate without Congressional oversight. The CRA has no enforcement mechanism, and to read it to preclude a court from reviewing whether an agency rule is in effect that should have been reported would render the statute ineffectual."[54] The court found that the post-enactment legislative history "buttresses the 'limited scope' of the CRA's judicial review provision" but was careful to acknowledge that "the lack of formal legislative history for the CRA makes reliance on this joint statement troublesome." However, the court made it clear that "this court reached its conclusion about the limited scope of the judicial review provision of the CRA based on the text of the statute and overall purpose of the act. The legislative history only serves to further reinforce the Court's conclusion."[55]

It is certainly arguable that the *Southern Indiana* court's view of the limited preclusiveness of Section 805 is plausible. A potentially stronger case can be made from a closer analysis of the text and structure of the act taken as a whole.

Although the court was correct as a general matter that post- enactment legislative history normally is given less weight, there are a number of Supreme Court rulings that recognize that under certain circumstances, arguably applicable here, contemporaneous explanations of key provisions' intent have been found to be an "authoritative guide" to a statute's construction. In one instance the Court relied on an explanation given eight years after the passage of the legislation.

The plain, overarching purpose of the review provision of the CRA was to assure that all covers final rulemaking actions of agencies would come before Congress for scrutiny.[56] The scheme provides for the delayed effectiveness of some rules deemed innately important ("major rules"), Section 801 (a)(3), and temporarily waives the submission requirement of Section 801 for rules establishing, modifying, opening, closing or conducting a regulatory program for a commercial, recreational, or subsistence activity related to hunting, fishing, or camping, or for a rule an agency "for good cause" finds that notice and public procedure are impractical, unnecessary, or contrary to the public interest. Section 808. Rules promulgated pursuant to the Telecommunications Act of 1996 are excluded from the definition of "major rule". But all such rules must ultimately be submitted for review. And while the scheme anticipates that some (or even most) rules will go into effect before a joint resolution of disapproval is passed, the law provides that enactment of a joint resolution terminates the effectiveness of the rule and that the rule will be treated as though it had never taken effect. Sections 801 (b)(1), 801(f). Further, a rule that has been nullified cannot be reissued by an agency in substantially the same form unless it is specifically authorized to do so by law after the date of the disapproval. Section 801 (b)(2).

The review scheme also requires a variety of actions by persons or agencies in support of the review process, and time for such actions to be scrutinized by both Houses to implement the scheme. Thus, the Comptroller General must submit a report to Congress on each major rule submitted within 15 calendar days after its submission or publication of the rule (Section 801(a)(2)(A)); the Administrator of OIRA determines whether a rule is a "major rule" (Section 804(2)); and after a rule is reported the Senate has 60 session days, and the House 60 legislative days, to pass a disapproval resolution under expedited procedures. Section 802. But Congress has preserved for itself a period of review of at least 60 session or legislative days. Therefore, if a rule is reported within 60 session days of the Senate (or 60 legislative days of the House) prior to the date Congress adjourns a session of the Congress, the period during which Congress may consider and pass a joint resolution of disapproval is extended to the next succeeding session of the Congress. Section 801(d)(1).

Thus the statutory scheme appears geared toward congressional review of all covered rules at some time; and a reading of the statute that allows for easy avoidance would seem to defeat that purpose. Interpreting the judicial review preclusion provision to prevent court scrutiny of the validity of administrative enforcement of covered but non-submitted rules appears to be neither a natural nor warranted reading of the provision. Section 805 speaks to "determination[s], finding[s], action[s], or omission[s] *under this chapter*," a plain reference to the range of actions authorized or required as part of the review process. Thus Congress arguably did not intend, as is more fully described below, to subject to judicial scrutiny, its own internal procedures, the validity of Presidential determinations that rules should become effective immediately for specified reasons, the propriety of OIRA determinations whether rules are major or not, or whether the Comptroller General properly performed his reporting function. These are matters that Congress can remedy by itself. From one perspective, the potential of court invalidation of enforcement actions based on the failure to submit covered rules, is necessary to assure compliance with submission requirements. If Section 805 is read so broadly, it would arguably render ineffective as well the Section 801 (b)(2) prohibition against an agency promulgating a new rule that is "substantially the same" as a disapproved rule unless it "is specifically reauthorized by a law enacted after" the passage of a disapproval resolution. It is more than likely that a determination whether a new or reissued rule is "substantially the same" as a disapproved rule is one that a court will be asked to make.[57] Congress appears to have contemplated (and approved) judicial review in this and other situations when it provided in Section 801(g) that "[i]f Congress does not enact a joint resolution of disapproval under section 802 respecting a rule, no court or agency may infer any interest of the Congress from any action or inaction of the Congress with regard to such rule, related statute, or joint resolution of disapproval."

The legislative history of the review provision confirms this view of the limited reach of the judicial review preclusion language. A key sponsor of the legislation, Representative McIntosh, explained during the floor debate on H.R. 3136 that "Under Section 8(a)(1)(A), covered rules may not go into effect until the relevant agency submits a copy of the rule and an accompanying report to both Houses of Congress."[58]

Shortly thereafter, the principal Senate and House sponsors of H.R. 3136 published a Joint Explanatory Statement in the Congressional Record providing a detailed explanation of the provisions of the congressional review provision of the CRA and its legislative history. Senator Nickles explained:

> Mr. NICKLES. Mr. President, I will submit for the RECORD a statement which serves to provide a detailed explanation and a legislative history for the congressional review title of H.R. 3136, the Small Business Regulatory Enforcement Fairness Act of 1996. H.R. 3136 was passed by the Senate on March 28, 1996, and was signed by the President the next day . . . Because title III of H.R. 3136 was the product of negotiation with the Senate and did not go through the committee process, no other expression of its legislative history exists other than the joint statement made by Senator REID and myself immediately before passage of H.R. 3136 on March 28. I am submitting a joint statement to be printed in the RECORD on behalf of myself, as the sponsor of the S. 219, Senator REID, the prime co-sponsor of S. 219, and Senator STEVENS, the chairman of the Committee on Governmental Affairs. This joint statement is intended to provide guidance to the agencies, the courts, and other interested parties when interpreting the act's terms. The same statement has been submitted today in the House by the chairmen of the committees of jurisdiction over the congressional review legislation.[59]

The Joint Explanatory Statement is clear as to the scope and limitation of the judicial review provision:

Limitation on judicial review of congressional or administrative actions

> Section 805 provides that a court may not review any congressional or administrative "determination, finding, action, or omission under this chapter". Thus, the major rule determinations made by the Administrator of the Office of Information and Regulatory Affairs of the Office of Management and Budget are not subject to judicial review. Nor may a court review whether Congress complied with the congressional review procedures in this chapter. This latter limitation on the scope of judicial review was drafted in recognition of the constitutional right of each House of Congress to "determine the Rules of its Proceedings". U.S. Const. art. I, §5, cl. 2, which includes each house being the final arbiter of compliance with such Rules.
>
> The limitation on a court's review of subsidiary determinations or compliance with congressional procedures, however, does not bar a court from giving effect to a resolution of disapproval that was enacted into law. A court with proper jurisdiction may treat the congressional enactment of a joint resolution of disapproval as it would treat the enactment of any other federal law. Thus, a court with proper jurisdiction may review the resolution of disapproval and the law that authorized the disapproved rule to determine whether the issuing agency has the legal authority to issue a substantially different rule. The language of subsection 801(g) is also instructive. Subsection 801(g) prohibits a court or agency from inferring any intent of the Congress only when "Congress does not enact a joint resolution of disapproval", or by implication, when it has not yet done so. In deciding cases

> or controversies properly before it, a court or agency must give effect to the intent of the Congress when such a resolution is enacted and becomes the law of the land. The limitation on judicial review in no way prohibits a court from determining whether a rule is in effect. For example, the authors expect that a court might recognize that a rule has no legal effect due to the operation of subsections 801(a)(1)(A) or 801(a)(3).[60]

The Justice Department has suggested that such post-enactment legislative history should not carry any weight, particularly in view of the unambiguous nature of the preclusion language at issue.[61] However, as discussed below, the courts appear to have taken a contrary view in analogous interpretive situations.

The Joint Explanatory Statement is a contemporaneous explanation of the congressional review provision by the legislative sponsors of the legislation which is consonant with the text and structure of the legislation. Such statements by legislative sponsors have been described by the Supreme Court as an "authoritative guide to the statute's construction." *North Haven Bd. of Education v. Bell*, 456 U.S. 512, 526-27 (1 982)(citing a bill summary placed in the Congressional Record by the bill's sponsor after passage, and explanatory remarks made two years later by the same sponsor); *Pacific Gas & Electric Co. v. Energy Resources Conservation and Development Commission,* 461 U.S. 190, 211 n. 23 (1983)(relying on a 1965 explanation by "an important figure in the drafting of the 1957 [Atomic Energy Act"]); *Grove City College v. Bell,* 465 U.S. 555, 567 (1984)(remarks of sponsors deemed authoritative when they are consistent with the language of the legislation).

Finally it may be noted that analogous preclusion of judicial review provisions in the original Paperwork Reduction Act of 1980, P.L. 96-511 and in the 1995 revision of the act, P.L. 104-13, have been uniformly construed by the courts to allow enforcement of its public protection provision. Thus 44 U.S.C. 3504 (1994), which authorized the Director of OMB to review and approve or disapprove information collection requirements in agency rules, and to assign control numbers to such forms, provided that "there shall be no judicial review of any kind of the Director's decision to approve or not to act upon a collection of information requirement contained in an agency rule." 44 U.S.C. 3504(h)(9). A similar provision appears in the 1995 revision of the Paperwork Reduction Act.[62] The 1980 legislation also contained a "public protection" provision which absolved a person from any penalty for not complying with an information collection request if the form did not display an OMB control number or failed to state that the request was not subject to the act.[63] The public protection provision, Section 3512, has been the subject of numerous court actions, some finding it applicable and providing a complete defense to noncompliance, others finding it inapplicable. But no court has ever raised a question with respect to preclusion of judicial review.[64]

A reviewing court construing the language of the congressional review provision, the structure of the legislation, and its legislative history, including post-enactment statements, is therefore could well hold that a court is not precluded from preventing an agency from enforcing a covered rule that was not reported to Congress in compliance with Section 801 (a)(1)(A).

7. The Uncertainty of the Breadth of the Prohibition Against an Agency's Promulgation of a "Substantially Similar" Rule after the Original Rule Has Been Vetoed

Enactment into law of a disapproval resolution has several important consequences. First, a disapproved rule is deemed not to have had any effect at any time. Thus, even a rule that has become effective for any period of time is retroactively negated.[65] Second, a rule that does not take effect, or is not continued because of the passage of a disapproval resolution, cannot be "reissued in the same form" nor can a "new rule" that is "substantially the same" as the disapproved rule be issued unless such action is specifically authorized by a law enacted subsequent to the disapproval of the original rule.[66] The full text of this provision states:

> (2) A rule that does not take effect (or does not continue) under paragraph (1) may not be reissued in substantially the same form, and a new rule that is substantially the same as such a rule may not be issued, unless the reissued or new rule is specifically authorized by a law enacted after the date of the joint resolution disapproving the original rule.

Finally, if a rule that is subject to any statutory, regulatory or judicial deadline for its promulgation is not allowed to take effect, or is terminated by the passage of a joint resolution, any deadline is extended for one year after the date of enactment of the disapproval resolution.[67]

Opponents of a disapproval resolution may argue that successful passage of a resolution may disable an agency from ever promulgating rules in the "area" covered by the resolution without future legislative reauthorization since a successful disapproval resolution must necessarily bring down the entire rule. Or, at the very least, it may be contended that any future attempt by the agency to promulgate new rules with respect to the subject matter will be subject to judicial challenge by regulated persons who may claim that either the new rules are substantially the same as those disapproved or that the statute provides no meaningful standard to discern whether a new rule is substantially the same and that the agency must await congressional guidance in the form of a statute before it can engage in further rulemaking in the area. The practical effect of these arguments, then, may be to dissuade an agency from taking any action until Congress provides clear authorization.

A review of the CRA's statutory scheme and structure, the contemporaneous congressional explanation of the legislative intent with respect to the provisions in question, the lessons learned from the experience of the March 2001 disapproval of the OSHA ergonomics rule, and the application of pertinent case law and statutory construction principles suggests that (1) It is doubtful that Congress intended that all disapproved rules would require statutory reauthorization before further agency action could take place. For example, it appears that Congress anticipated further rulemaking, without new authorization, where the statute in question established a deadline for promulgating implementing rules in a particular area. In such instances, the CRA extends the deadline for promulgation for one year from the date of disapproval. (2) A close reading of the statute, together with its contemporaneous congressional explication, arguably provides workable standards for agencies to reform disapproved regulations that are likely to be taken into account by reviewing courts. Those standards would require a reviewing court to assess both the nature of the rulemaking authority vested in the agency that promulgated the disapproved rule and the specificity with which the Congress identified the objectionable portions of a rule during the floor debates on disapproval. An important factor in a judicial assessment may be the CRA's recognition of the continued efficacy of statutory deadlines for promulgating specified rules by extending such deadlines for one year after disapproval. (3) The novelty of the issue, the uncertainty of the weight a court may accord the post enactment congressional explanation, and the current judicial inclination to give deference to the "plain meaning" of legislative language, make it difficult to anticipate what a court is likely to hold.

Since Congress can apparently only disapprove a rule as a whole, rather than pinpointing any particular portions, there may be no sound basis for the agency to act without further legislative guidance where a rule deals exclusively with an integrated subject matter. The statute gives no indication as to how an agency is to discern what actions would be "substantially the same" and it would run the risk of a successful court challenge if it guessed wrong. It might be further argued that even if the agency promulgates new rules, which of course would be subject to CRA scrutiny, and Congress did not act to disapprove the new rules, that would not provide the necessary reauthorization since Section 801(g) of the act provides as a rule of construction that in the event of the failure of Congress to disapprove a rule "no court ... may infer any intent of Congress from any action or inaction of the Congress with regard to such, related statute, or joint resolution of disapproval."

It is fundamental that statutory language is the starting point in any case of statutory construction. In recent years, the Supreme Court has shown a strong disposition to hold Congress to the letter of the language it uses in its enactments. In its ruling in *Barnhart v. Sigmon Coal Co.[68]* the Court advised that the first step "is to determine whether the language at issue has a plain and unambiguous meaning with regard to the particular dispute in the case."[69] "The inquiry ceases 'if the statutory language is unambiguous and the statutory scheme is coherent and consistent.'"[70] In such cases, the Court has held, resort to "legislative history is irrelevant to the interpretation of an unambiguous statute."[71] In *Barnhardt* the Court warned, "parties should not seek to amend [a] statute by appeal to the Judicial Branch."[72]

The plain meaning rule, however, is not an unalterable, rigid rule of construction and has been held inapplicable where it would "lead to an absurd result,"[73] or "would bring about an end completely at variance with the purpose of the statute."[74] "It is 'a fundamental canon of statutory construction that the words of a statute must be read in their context and with a view to their place in the overall statutory scheme' ... Thus it is a more faithful construction of [a statute] to read it as a whole, rather than as containing two unrelated parts. It is the classic judicial task of construing related statutory provisions to make sense in combination."[75] In the instant situation, it is arguably not likely that a court would hold that the "substantially the same" language of Section 801 (b)(2) is unambiguous, either on its face or in the context of the statutory scheme. The direction of the provision is not a self-enforcing mandate; it clearly requires a further determination whether rules have been reissued in "substantially the same form" or whether a new rule is "substantially the same" as the one disapproved. The ambiguity raised appears to be who makes those determinations and on what basis.

The language of the provision, however, does not naturally or ineluctably lead to the conclusion that no further remedial rulemaking can take place unless Congress passes a new law. This reasoning is buttressed by Section 803(a) which contemplates that agency rulemaking must take place after a disapproval action if the authorizing legislation of the agency mandates that rules disapproved had to have been promulgated by a date certain. That provision extends the deadline for promulgation for one year "after the date of enactment of the joint resolution," not one year after Congress reauthorizes action in the area. A reasonable conclusion is that Congress understood that after disapproval, an agency, if it was under a mandate to produce a particular rule, had to try again. The question then is, how was it to perform this task. The answer may lie in the legislative history of the act.

The Congressional Review Act was part of Title II of the Small Business Regulatory Enforcement Fairness Act of 1996. That Title was a product of negotiation between the Senate and House and did not go through the committee process. Thus there is no detailed expression of its legislative history, apart from floor statements by key House and Senate sponsors, before its passage by the Congress on March 28, 1996 and its signing into law by the President on March 29. Thereafter, the principal sponsors of the legislation in the Senate (Senators Nickles, Reid and Stevens) and House (Representative Hyde) submitted identical joint explanatory statements for publication in the Congressional Record "intended to provide guidance to the agencies, the courts, and other interested parties when interpreting the act's terms."[76] Although it is a post-enactment explanation of the legislation, it is likely to be accorded some weight as a contemporaneous, detailed, in-depth statement of purpose and intent by the principal sponsors of the law.[77]

The Joint Explanatory Statement directly addresses a number of issues that may arise upon enactment of a disapproval resolution and attempts to provide guidance for both Congress and agencies faced with repromulgation questions. At the outset, the Statement notes that disapprovals may have differing impacts on promulgating agencies depending on the nature and scope the rulemaking authority that was utilized. For example, if an agency's authorizing legislation did not mandate the promulgation of the disapproved rule, and the legislation gives the agency broad discretion, the authors deem it likely that it has the discretion whether or not to promulgate a new rule. On the other hand, the Statement explains that "if an agency is mandated to promulgate a particular rule and its discretion is narrowly circumscribed, the enactment of a resolution of disapproval for that rule may work to prohibit the reissuance of any rule."[78] Arguably, a congressional mandate to issue regulations that is not narrowly focused would still be operative. But how would the agency be guided in that circumstance? The Statement addresses that very question: it is the obligation of Congress during the debate on the disapproval resolution "to focus on the law that authorized the rule and make the congressional intent clear regarding the agency's options or lack thereof after the enactment of a joint resolution of disapproval."[79] Thereafter, "the agency must give effect to the resolution of disapproval."[80] The full statement on the issue is as follows:

> Effect of enactment of a joint resolution of disapproval Subsection 801(b)(1) provides that "A rule shall not take effect (or continue), if the Congress enacts a joint resolution of disapproval, described under section

> 802, of the rule." Subsection 801(b)(2) provides that such a disapproval rule "may not be reissued in substantially the same form, and a new rule that is substantially the same as such a rule may not be issued, unless the reissued or new rule is specifically authorized by a law enacted after the date of the joint resolution disapproving the original rule." Subsection 801(b)(2) is necessary to prevent circumvention of a resolution disapproval. Nevertheless, it may have a different impact on the issuing agencies depending on the nature of the underlying law that authorized the rule.
>
> If the law that authorized the disapproved rule provides broad discretion to the issuing agency regarding the substance of such rule, the agency may exercise its broad discretion to issue a substantially different rule. If the law that authorized the disapproved rule did not mandate the promulgation of any rule, the issuing agency may exercise its discretion not to issue any new rule. Depending on the law that authorized the rule, an issuing agency may have both options. But if an agency is mandated to promulgate a particular rule and its discretion in issuing the rule is narrowly circumscribed, the enactment of a resolution of disapproval for that rule may work to prohibit the reissuance of any rule. The authors intend the debate on any resolution of disapproval to focus on the law that authorized the rule and make the congressional intent clear regarding the agency's options or lack thereof after enactment of a joint resolution of disapproval. It will be the agency's responsibility in the first instance when promulgating the rule to determine the range of discretion afforded under the original law and whether the law authorizes the agency to issue a substantially different rule. Then, the agency must give effect to the resolution of disapproval.

The congressional experience with the disapproval of the OSHA ergonomics standard provides a useful lesson. This rule became the first, and only, rule to be disapproved thus far under the CRA. The principal sponsor of the resolution, Senator Jeffords, at the outset of the debate addressed the issue whether disapproval would disable OSHA from promulgating a new rule. Senator Jeffords referred to the above- discussed Joint Statement and noted that OSHA "has enormously broad regulatory authority," citing pertinent sections of the OSH Act providing expansive rulemaking authority. The Senator concluded that "I am convinced that the CRA will not act as an impediment to OSHA *should* the agency decide to engage in ergonomics rulemaking."[81] What Senator Jeffords apparently understood was that while the agency had broad authority to promulgate rules, there was no congressional mandate to issue an ergonomics rule in the underlying law. As a consequence it was possible that no further rulemaking would occur, as implied by a letter to Senator Jeffords from Secretary Chao which indicated that a new rulemaking was only one of many options available to the Department should the rule be disapproved.[82] OSHA made it clear on April 5, 2002, that no rulemaking was in the offing. On April 17, 2002, Senator Breaux and 26 co-sponsors, many of whom had voted in favor of the disapproval resolution, introduced S. 2184, which would direct the Secretary of Labor to promulgate a new ergonomics rule and specifies in detail what should be included, what should not be included, and what evidence should be considered. Section 1 (b)(4) of the bill deems the direction to issue the rule "a specific authorization by Congress in accordance with Section 801 (b)(2)" of the CRA.

An interesting contrast with the ergonomics situation was the consideration given by the key Senate sponsors of the Bipartisan Campaign Reform Act 2002 (BCRA),[83] which required that the Federal Election Commission (FEC) promulgate rules implementing the soft money limitations and prohibitions of Title I of the act no later than 90 days after its date of enactment,[84] whether to introduce a CRA disapproval resolution with respect to the rules issued by the FEC on July 17, 2002.[85] The Senate sponsors believed that the new rules, which became effective on November 6, 2002, undermined the BCRA's ban on the raising and spending of soft money by federal candidates and officeholders and on national party use of soft money. Since the FEC was mandated to promulgate rules to implement the BCRA by a date certain, it could have been argued that, in contrast with the general discretion OSHA has with respect to whether to issue any ergonomics standard, if Congress disapproved the FEC's soft money rule, the agency would be obligated to undertake a new rulemaking (to be completed within a year after the disapproval resolution was signed into law) that would reflect congressional objections to the rule. At the same time, in accordance with the understanding of the Joint Statement, it would have been arguably incumbent on Congress in its debates on any such resolution to clearly identify those provisions of the rule that were objectionable as well as those that are not.

Whether this line of argument would suffice to withstand a challenge in the courts cannot be answered with any degree of certainty. Foreseeable obstacles may be the novelty of the issue, the amount of weight, if any, that a court will accord the post-enactment congressional explanation of the CRA, and the current inclination of the courts to give deference to the plain meaning of statutory language and to eschew legislative history. A new rule may be challenged on grounds of lack of authority as a consequence of the disapproval resolution either because Congress failed to articulate its objections to the rule, thereby providing no standards for the agency to apply in its rulemaking, or that the new rules were "substantially the same" as the old, disapproved rules and therefore invalid under the CRA.

The Joint Statement declares that it is the congressional intent to make clear and specific identification of the options available to the agency, including identification of objectionable provisions in the proposed rule during the floor debates. In this way

Congress could provide an agency clear and direct guidance as to what it expects in the repromulgation process as well as a possible defense to a challenge based on the "substantially the same" language of the CRA.

RECENT DEVELOPMENTS

In 2006 and 2007 suggestions for at least modest legislative remediation of the perceived flaws in the CRA, if for no other reason than to maintain a credible presence in the process of delegated administrative lawmaking, were presented in a number of forums. These included hearings held by the House Judiciary Subcommittee on Commercial and Administrative Law, a symposium held by the Congressional Research Service (CRS Symposium), CRS and GAO reports, published recommendations of the House Judiciary Subcommittee, and academic writings.[86] Participating witnesses and panelists concurred that the role of Congress as the nation's dominant policy maker was being threatened by widespread agency evasion of notice and comment rulemaking requirements; the continued pressure for legislative enhancement of the trend toward substantive judicial review of agency rules; and the frequent calls for increased presidential control of agency rulemaking.

In particular, studies characterizing current rulemaking procedures as ossified concluded that rule promulgation has become too time consuming, burdensome, and unpredictable. The thrust of the academic critics, which assigns blame to each of the branches for the increasingly ineffective implementation of statutory mandates, often identifies that courts as the chief culprits because of intrusion in agency decisionmaking through interpretations and applications of APA's arbitrary and capricious test. [87] Reviewing courts, it was maintained, will now find an agency to have violated its duty to engage in reasoned decisionmaking if its statement of basis and purpose is found to contain any gap in data or flaw in stated reasoning with respect to any issue. The commentators cite statistical indications that reviewing courts have been holding major rules invalid up to fifty percent of the time.[88] Preliminary indications of a study commissioned by the House Judiciary Subcommittee, however, appears to suggest a far less successful challenge rate, but the consequence of the perceived actions of the reviewing courts has been the encouragement of agencies to utilize alternative vehicles to make and announce far-reaching regulatory decisions.[89] It was also argued that agencies can use actions such as in adjudication of individual disputes or by so-called "non-rule" rules, where purportedly non-binding statements of policy are made in guidances, operating manuals, staff instructions, or like agency public communications.[90] However, the proposed solutions of these scholars are essentially adjurations to the judiciary to modify or abandon current doctrinal courses. For example, some scholars suggest that courts abolish the duty to engage in reasoned decision making and instead conduct a review of rules to determine whether they violate clear statutory or constitutional constraints, or apply the *Chevron* defense more consistently and strictly.[91]

It was also argued that only part of the problem facing Congress is fixing identifiable structural and interpretive flaws. Part may also be attributable to a lack of interest in confronting and dealing with complex and sensitive policy issues that major rulemakings often present. During the CRS-sponsored symposium on "Presidential, Congressional, and Judicial Control of Rulemaking", one panelist, Professor Jack Beermann, expressed his view that making it easier for Congress to overturn an agency rule may come at a high political cost. He asked "Does Congress want to be in the position where [it is perceived] that everything an agency does is their responsibility since they've taken it on and Reviewed it under this mechanism?. . .Do they want to have that perception?" He concluded that "I think that this may just increase the blaming opportunities for Congress."

Some of the commentators saw a failure of the Congress to understand and appreciate the nature of the stakes involved and the dangers inherent in failing to act decisively to resolve them. Professor Cynthia Farina argued that it was the legitimacy of the administrative lawmaking process that is at the heart of the deossification, nondelegation and new presidentialism debates. Her insight as to the necessity of viewing the legitimacy and operational effectiveness of the regulatory process as a "collaborative enterprise" involving the appropriate official actors and institutional practices may be seen by some as an informing guidepost for action.[92]

The following list of legislative options propounded by the House Judiciary Subcommittee in its "Interim Report"[93] appears based on propositions and assumptions extracted from the hearings held by the Committee on the CRA, the CRS symposium, CRS and GAO reports, and academic commentary:

1 Amend the CRA to provide that all covered rules must be submitted to Congress and cannot become effective until Congress passes a joint resolution of approval. This would vest significant control (as well as accountability) over agency rulemaking in Congress. It would require expedited consideration procedures be established in both Houses as well as a special process to assure speedy approval of non-

controversial proposed rules. Testimony before the Committee indicated that a "deeming" process could be established under the rulemaking authority of each House which would allow summary approval of all rules for which there has been no indication of a need for full consideration by the House, i.e., the filing of a notice of intent by a specific number of Members with a prescribed time period after congressional receipt of the proposed rule.[94] Although the internal decisional processes (expedited consideration and the deeming process) could be established by House rule, the requirement of congressional approval of all rules would require the passage of a new law. Presidential approval of such legislation is likely to be highly problematic.

2 By rule of each House establish a joint committee to act as a clearinghouse and screening mechanism for all covered rules. Such a committee would be advisory only, reporting to jurisdictional committees for both Houses its findings with respect to reported rules and recommendations, when appropriate, for action on joint resolutions of disapproval. The House of Representatives would establish by rule an expedited consideration procedure complimentary to the current Senate procedure. The joint committee would be authorized to request reports on submitted rules from GAO assessing such matters as the cost and benefits, cost effectiveness, and legal authority of the subject rule. None of the foregoing would require the passage of legislation requiring presidential approval.[95] The witnesses at the Committee's hearings and panelists at the CRS symposium concluded that the establishment of a joint congressional committee to screen rules and recommend action to jurisdictional committees in both Houses could provide the coordination and information necessary to inform both bodies sufficiently and in a timely manner to allow them to take actions under current law. The balanced nature of such a joint committee and its lack of substantive authority might provide a way to allay political concerns regarding "turf" intrusions.

3 Amend the CRA to direct that reports to Congress and GAO of covered rules are to be submitted electronically. The House Parliamentarian and other witnesses and symposium panelists indicated that the paperwork burden on the Parliamentarian's office as well as the uncertainties of proper receipt by Congress and timely redirection to the appropriate committees, and other problems with paper submissions, could be relieved by electronic submissions.

4 Amend the CRA to require the reporting of only "major rules." This option was suggested by witnesses and panelists as a means limiting the screening burden on committees and on the assumption that only "major rules" are likely to raise significant congressional review issues. At present, the CRA allows only the Administrator of OIRA to designate which rules are to be deemed "major." However, even a rule that may be conceded to be "minor," in the sense of it having minimal economic impact, may well have a significance to congressional constituencies. The difficulty would be designating a determiner that is politically acceptable and constitutionally appropriate. The Supreme Court's ruling in INS v. Chadha,[96] the legislative veto case, precludes authorizing legislative committees or officers from selecting particular rules and ordering agencies to report them for review. In view of the practical and legal problems, it may well be that the current requirement of blanket rule reporting, perhaps supplemented by a screening body, such as the suggested joint committee, would be more acceptable.

5 Amend the CRA to make it clear that failing to report a covered rule renders the rule unenforceable and is subject to judicial review. Proponents of the CRA consider this lack of an enforceable reporting requirement to undermine the purpose of the CRA.

6 Amend the CRA to make it clear that an up-or-down vote is on the entire reported rule. The credible threat of congressional review would presumably force agencies to carefully tailor their rules with more attention to congressional expectations. Expedition in the review process, however, is vital so as not to undermine agency enforcement and the certainty needed by the regulated community. The possibility of conflicting disapproval resolutions from each House, and long, perhaps unsuccessful conference committees deliberations, may undermine the intended purpose of the CRA. The following option, however, may ameliorate the concern over the up-or-down vote on the entire rule.

7 Amend the CRA to provide that if a rule is disapproved, an agency is prohibited from repromulgating only those provisions of the rule that the review process and floor debates on disapproval clearly identify as objectionable. Such a qualification to the CRA review process appears to comport with the legislative intent of the sponsors of the CRA. If the option of creation of a joint committee were adopted, it could be mandated to identify the discrete problems of the rule that were objectionable. That would obviate the necessity of legislative amendment to reestablish agency authority in an area after passage of a disapproval resolution.

CONCLUSION

This chapter identifies structural and interpretive issues affecting use of the CRA. While there have been some instances of the law apparently influencing the implementation of certain rules, the limited utilization of the formal disapproval process in the ten years since enactment has arguably reduced the threat of possible congressional scrutiny and disapproval as a factor in agency rule development. The one instance in which an agency rule was successfully negated is likely a singular event not soon to be repeated. Presently, the Congress and the White House are in the hands of opposing political partys, the rules of the previous Administration are no longer subject to the CRA, and the current Administration appears to be establishing firm control of the agency rulemaking process through its administration of Executive Order 12,866.[97] One commentator opined that if the perception of a rulemaking agency is that the possibility of congressional review is remote "it will discount the likelihood of congressional intervention because of the uncertainty about where Congress might stand on that rule when it is promulgated years down the road," an attitude that is reinforced "so long as [the agency] believes that the president will support its rule."[98] Some observers say that a significant number of covered rules is not being submitted for review at all. Also, a potentially effective support mechanism, the in-depth, individualized scrutiny of selected agency cost-benefit and risk assessment analyses by GAO authorized under the Truth in Regulating Act of 2000, was never implemented for lack of appropriated funds.

SELECTED SOURCE READINGS

Cohen, Daniel and Strauss, Peter L. "Congressional Review of Agency Regulations." *Administrative Law Review* 49 (Winter 1996): 95-110.

Parks, Julia A. "Lessons in Politics: Initial Use of the Congressional Review Act." *Administrative Law Review* 55 (Fall 2003): 187-210.

Pfohl, Peter A. "Congressional Review of Agency Rulemaking: The 104th Congress and the Salvage Timber Directive." *14 Journal of Law and Politics* (Winter 1998): 1-31.

Rosenberg, Morton. "Whatever Happened to Congressional Review of Agency Rulemaking?: A Brief Overview, Assessment, and Proposal for Reform." *51 Administrative Law Review* (Fall 1999): 1051-1092.

U.S. Congress. "Interim Report on the Administrative Law, Process, and Procedure Project for the 21st Century." House Judiciary Committee, Subcommittee on Commercial and Administrative Law, 109th Cong., 2d Sess. (December 2006)(Committee Print No. 10).

References

[1] Section 804(3) excludes from the definition "(A) any rule of particular applicability, including a rule that approves or prescribes for the future rates, wages, prices, services, or allowance therefore, corporate or financial structures, reorganizations, mergers, or acquisitions thereof, or accounting practices or disclosures bearing on any of the foregoing; (B) any rule relating to agency management or personnel; or (C) any rule of agency organization, or practice that does not substantially affect the rights or obligations on non- agency parties."

[2] Attorney General's Manual on the Administrative Procedure Act 13 (1948).

[3] *Avoyelles Sportmsmen 's League, Inc., v. Marsh,* 715 F.2d 897 (5th Cir. 1983).

[4] See, e.g., *Chem Service, Inc. v. EPA,* 12 F.3d 1256 (3d Cir. 1993)(memorandum of understanding); *Caudill v. Blue Cross and Blue Shield of North Carolina,* 999 F.2d 74 (4th Cir. 1 993)(interpretative rules); *National Treasury Employees Union v. Reagan*, 685 F.Supp 1346 (E.D. La 1988)(federal personnel manual letter issued by OPM); *New York City Employment Retirement Board v. SEC,* 45 F.3d 7 (2d Cir. 1995)(affirming lower court's ruling that SEC "no action" letter was a rule within section 551(4)).

[5] The General Counsel of the Government Accountability Office (GAO) has ruled that the 60-day period does not begin to run until *both* Houses of Congress receive the required report. See B-289880, April 5, 2002, opinion letter to Hon. Edward M. Kennedy, Chairman, Senate Committee on Health, Education, Labor and Pensions from Anthony H. Gamboa, General Counsel. The situation involved a Department of Health and Human Service's (HHS) major rule published in the Federal Register on January 18, 2002 with an announced effective date of March 29, 2002. The House of Representatives, however, did not receive the rule until February 14, 2002. HHS thereafter delayed the effective date of the rule until April 15, 2002, in an attempt to comply with the CRA. But the Senate did not receive the rule until March 15,

2002. The General Counsel determined that the rule could not become effective until May 14, 2002, 60 days following the Senate's receipt, relying on the language of Section 801(a)(1)(A) of the act requiring that a copy of a covered rule must be be submitted "to *each* House of Congress" in order to become effective.

[6] Reviewing courts have generally applied the Administrative Procedure Act's good cause exemption, from which this language is obviously taken, narrowly in order to prevent agencies from using it as an escape clause from notice and comment requirements. See, e.g., *Action* on *Smoking and Health v. CAS,* 713 F.2d 795, 800 (D.C. Cir. 1987). However, since Section 805 precludes judicial review for any "determination, finding, action or omission under this chapter", there could be no court condemnation of a good cause determination. But the rule would still be subject to congressional vacation and retroactive nullification.

[7] In *Leisegang v. Sect 'y of Veterans Affairs*, 312 F.3d 1368, 1373-1376 (Fed. Cir. 2002), the appeals court held that Section 801(a)(3) "does not change the date on which [a major rule] becomes effective. It only affects the date when the rule becomes operative. In other words, the CRA merely provides a 60-day waiting period before the agency may enforce the major rule so that Congress has the opportunity to review the regulation." At issue in the case was the date from which certain veterans benefits would be calculated. The benefit statute provided that it would be the date of the issuance of the rule. The government argued that the CRA was a superceding statute and that the effective date was when the CRA allowed it to be operative. The appeals court agreed with the veterans that the date of issuance, as prescribed by the law, was determinative.

[8] For an in-depth discussion of procedural issues that may arise during House and Senate consideration of disapproval resolutions, see Richard S. Beth, CRS Report RL3 1160, *Disapproval of Regulations by Congress: Procedure Under the Congressional Review Act*, October10, 2001 (Archived).

[9] There is some question whether a motion to proceed is nondebatable because of the absence of language so stating. Arguably, the nondebatability of the motion is integral both to the scheme of the expedited procedure provisions as well as to the overall efficacy of the CRA's statutory scheme and thus may be implied. Alternatively, debate on such a motion may be limited by Section 803(d)(2) which limits debate on joint resolutions, as well as "all debatable motions," to 10 hours. Ultimately, a resolution of this question would be made by the Senate Parliamentarian, or the Senate itself. However, at the commencement of the debate on S.J.Res. 6, to disapprove the

ergonomics rule, the presiding officer declared that "The motion to proceed is not debatable. The question is on agreeing to the motion." The motion was agreed to. 147 Cong. Rec. S 1831 (daily ed. March 6, 2001). At least one other precedent exists in which it was ruled that a motion to proceed to a budget resolution under the Budget Act was nondebatable despite the silence of the act on the matter. *See,* 127 Cong. Rec. S 4871 (May 12, 1981).

[10] See discussion *infra* at pp 24-29.

[11] General Accounting Office, Reports on Federal Agency Major Rules, which may be found at [http://www.gao.gov/decisions/majrule/majrule.htm].

[12] In a close floor vote, the rider proposed for FY 1997 was deleted.

[13] 65 Fed. Reg. 68261 (2000).

[14] P.L. 107-5.

[15] P.L. 105-78.

[16] See Allan Freedman, "GOP's Secret Weapon Against Regulations: Finesse," *CQ Weekly*, September 5, 1998, at 23 18-19 (Freedman).

[17] Freedman, *supra* note 17, at 23 19-20.

[18] *See* 142 Cong. Rec. S 10723 (daily ed. September 17, 1996).

[19] 29 Weekly Comp. Pres. Doc. 88 (1993).

[20] 22 U.S.C. 2151b(b) and b(f)(1) (2000).

[21] 37 Weekly Comp. Pres. Doc. 216 (2001).

[22] Compare *Franklin v. Massachusetts*, 505 U.S. 788, 800 (1992) and *Dalton v. Specter*, 511 U.S. 462, 469 (1994), holding that the President is not subject to APA procedures since he is not expressly covered by its definition of agency, with *Chamber of Commerce v. Reich*, 74 F.3d 1311 (D.C. Cir. 1998) and *National Family Planning Council v. Sullivan*, 979 F.2d 227 (D.C. Cir. 1992), allowing challenges to agency rules that were issued pursuant to presidential directive.

[23] See, Restoration of the Mexico City Policy: Memorandum for the Administrator of the U.S. Agency for International Development, March 28, 2001, 66 *Fed. Reg.* 17303-17313 (March 29, 2001).

[24] A companion bill, S. 1675, was introduced in the Senate by Senators Shelby and Bond. 143 Cong. Rec. S1007 (daily ed. February 25, 1998).

[25] See H.Rept. 105-441, Parts 1 and 2 (105th Cong., 2d Sess.) (1998).

[26] Section 4 (a)(3)(A).

[27] P.L. 106-312, 114 Stat. 1248-50, 5 U.S.C. 801 note.

[28] See introductory remarks on the measure at 147 Cong. Rec. H 2454 (daily ed. October 21, 2003).

[29] The experience with respect to the repeal of the ergonomics standard, discussed supra at 12-13, would appear to bear this out.

[30] See, Mark Seidenfeld, The Psychology of Accountability and Political Review of Agency Rules, 51 Duke L.J. 1059, 1089 (2001).

[31] S.J.Res. 17, dealing with the FCC's media ownership rule, which passed in the Senate but was not acted upon in the House.

[32] See e.g., Reorganization Act Amendments of 1984, providing that both Houses of Congress had to pass a joint resolution approving a reorganization plan within 90 days of continuous session after the date of presidential submission or else it is deemed disapproved. 5 U.S.C. 906 (a) (1994).

[33] Two bills introduced in the 1 06th Congress to revise the CRA utilized the joint resolution of approval approach. See S. 1348, 106th Cong., 1st Sess. (1999)(Sen. Brownback) S. 2670, 106th Cong., 2nd Sess. (2000)(Sen. Thomas). A similar approach was reflected in H.R. 110 introduced by Rep. Hayworth (with 25 co-sponsors) in the 108th Congress.

[34] E.g., S.J.Res. 50 and H.J.Res. 123, "relating to surety bond requirements for home health agencies under the medicare and medicaid programs...."

[35] Joint Explanatory Statement of House and Senate Sponsors, 142 Cong. Rec. E 571, at E 577 (daily ed. April 19, 1996); 142 Cong. Rec. S 3683, at S 3686 (daily ed. April 18, 1996)(Legislative History)(emphasis added). These identical detailed explanations by the legislative sponsors of the intent and scope of the CRA's provisions appeared in the daily editions of the Congressional Record some three weeks after SBREFA was signed into law. In the absence of committee hearings and the sparse commentary during floor debate, these explanations represent the most authoritative contemporary understanding of the provisions of the law. It is, however, post-enactment legislative history and does not carry the weight that committee report explanations and floor debates provide. As one court dealing with the interpretation of a CRA provision stated, the post-enactment legislative history "buttresses the 'limited scope' of the CRA judicial review provision" but warned that "the lack of formal legislative history for the CRA makes reliance on this joint statement troublesome." See *United States v. Southern Indiana Gas & Electric Co*, discussed *infra* at note 54 and accompanying text. The permanent edition of the Congressional Record for the 1 04th Congress places the Senate sponsors Joint Explanation at April 18, 1996, the same date it appeared in daily edition. See 142 Cong. Rec. 8196-8201. The House sponsors' Joint Explanation, which originally appeared in the daily edition of April 19, 1996, is now placed during the floor debate on SBREFA on March 28, 1996, the date of its passage. See 142

Cong. Rec. 6922-6930. There is no explanation for the earlier placement. As a consequence, we have determined to continue to treat the Joint Explanation as post- enactment legislative history. See discussion at *infra*, at pp. 27-33.

[36] Defense Base Closure and Realignment Act of 1990, P.L. 101-510, sec. 2908 (b) 104 Stat. 1808, in note following 10 U.S.C. 2687 (2000).

[37] See, 19 U.S.C. 2191-2193 (2000).

[38] See, e.g., Reorganization Act of 1984, 5 U.S.C. 909-9 12 (2000).

[39] See footnotes 1-4, *supra*, and accompanying text.

[40] Join Explanatory Statement of House and Senate sponsors, *supra* n. 35, at E 579, S 3687.

[41] This practice has been long recognized and criticized in administrative law commentaries. See, e.g., Robert A. Anthony, Interpretive Rules, Policy Statements, Guidances, Manuals, and the Like — Should Federal Agencies Use Them To Bind The Public?, 41 Duke L.J. 1311 (1992). Cf. also, General Accounting Office, Federal Rulemaking: Agencies Often Published Final Actions Without Proposed Rules, GAO/GGD-98-126 (August 1998).

[42] Legislative History, *supra* n. 35, at E 578, S 3687.

[43] An investigation by the House Subcommittee on National Economic Growth, Natural Resources, and Regulatory Affairs (Government Reform) which revealed that 7,523 guidance documents issued by the Department of Labor, the Environmental Protection Agency, and the Department of Transportation which were of general applicability and future effect had not been submitted for CRA review during the period March 1996 through November 1999. See "Non-Binding Legal Effect of Agency Guidance Documents," [http://www.congress.gov/cgi-lis/cpquery/T?&report=hr1 009& db name=cp 1 06&] H.Rept. 106-1009, 106th Cong., 2nd Sess. (2000).

[44] P.L. 105-277, Division A, title III.

[45] See [http://www.congress.gov/cgi-lis/cpquery/T?&report=hr1 009&dbname= cp 1 06&] H.Rept. 106-1009, *supra* n. 44 at 4-5.

[46] See letter dated June 11, 1997 to the Honorable Lamar Smith, Chairman, Subcommittee on Immigration and Claims, Senate Judiciary Committee, from Andrew Fois, Assistant Attorney General, Office of Legislative Affairs, DOJ, and accompanying analysis dated June 10, 1997, at pp 9-11 (DOJ Memorandum).

[47] 1998 U.S. Dist. LEXIS 13470, 1998 WL842 181 (W. Texas), aff'd 201 F.3d 551 (5th Cir. 2000).

[48] Id. at note 15.

[49] 218 F.Supp. 3d 931 (S.D. Ohio 2002).

[50] For background on the legal development of the issue, see CRS Report RS2 1424, *Air Pollution: Legal Perspective on the 'Routine Maintenance' Exception to New Source Review*, by Robert Meltz (Archived).

[51] 218 F.Supp. 2d at 949.

[52] *Id.*

[53] 2002 U.S. Dist. LEXIS 20936; 55 ERC (BNA) 1597 (D.C. S.D. Ind. 2002).

[54] 2002 U.S. Dist. LEXIS 20936 at 13-14.

[55] *Id.* at 15-16 and note 3.

[56] "This legislation establishes a government-wide congressional review mechanism for most new rules. This allows Congress the opportunity to review a rule before it takes effect and to disapprove any rule to which Congress objects." Legislative History, *supra* note 35, at E 575 and S 3683.

[57] The disapproval of the ergonomics rule underlines a possible need for judicial review in certain instances where enforcement is necessary and appropriate to support the statutory scheme. That rule, which was broad and encompassing in its regulatory scope, raises the question as to how far can the agency go before it reaches the point of substantial similarity in its promulgation of a substitute. This issue is addressed in the next section.

[58] 142 Cong. Rec. H3005 (daily ed. March 28, 1996).

[59] Legislative History, *supra* note 35, at 142 Cong. Rec. S 3683.

[60] *Id.,* at E 577 and S 3686.

[61] See DOJ memorandum, *supra* n. 47, at 10 n.14.

[62] 44 U.S.C. 3507(d)(6)(2000).

[63] See 44 U.S.C. 3512 (1994).

[64] Compare *United States v. Smith*, 866 F.2d 1092 (9th Cir. 1 980)(failure of Forest Service to file a plan of operations with OMB control number precluded conviction for failure to file) and *Cameron v. IRS*, 593 F.Supp. 1540, *aff'd* 773 F.2d 126 (6th Cir. 1984)(failure of IRS forms to have OMB control numbers did not violate section since it was a collection of information during the investigation of a specific individual or entity which is exempt under the provision).

[65] 5 U.S.C. 801(f).

[66] 5 U.S.C. 801(b)(2).

[67] 5 U.S.C. 803.

[68] 534 U.S. 438 (2002).

[69] *Id.* at 450.

[70] *Id.*

[71] *Davis v. Michigan Dept. of Treasury*, 489 U.S. 803, 808-09 n.3. *Accord Connecticut National Bank v. Germain*, 503 U.S. 249, 253-54 (1992); *United States v.Daas*, 198 F.2d 1167, 1175 (9th Cir. 1999), *cert. denied* 531 U.S. 999 (2000).

[72] 534 U.S. at 462..

[73] *Holy Trinity Church v. United States*, 143 U.S. 457, 459 (1892).

[74] *United Steelworkers v. Weber*, 443 U.S. 193, 201 (1978).

[75] *United States v. Wilson*, 290 F.3d 347 (D.C. Cir. 2002) (holding, *inter alia*, that it is appropriate for a court to look at the history and background against which Congress was legislating).

[76] Legislative History, *supra*, n. 35.

[77] See e.g., *North Haven Bd. of Education v. Bell*, 456 U.S. 512, 530-31 (1982); *Pacific Gas & Electric Co. v. Energy Resources Conservation & Development Commission*, 461 U.S. 190, 220 n.23 (1983); *Grove City College* v. *Bell* , 465 U.S. 555, 567 (1984).

[78] Legislative History *supra* note 35 at S 3686.

[79] *Id.*

[80] *Id.*

[81] 147 Cong. Rec. S 1832-33 (daily ed. March 6, 2001) (emphasis added).

[82] 147 Cong. Rec. at S 1832.

[83] P.L. 107-55, 116 Stat. 81 (March 27, 2002).

[84] Section 402 (c)(2).

[85] Kenneth P. Doyle, Wertheimer, Bauer Debate Move to Void Soft Money Rule Before Senate Democrats, Bureau of National Affairs, July 19, 2002. A disapproval resolution of the FEC rules was introduced in the Senate, S.J.Res. 48, on October 8, 2002, but was never acted upon by either House.

[86] See Interim Report on "The Administrative Law, Process, and Procedure Project for the 21st Century." House Subcommittee on Commercial and Administrative Law, Judiciary Committee, 1 09th Cong. 2d Sess. (December 2006)(Committee Print No. 10); Hearing, (Reauthorization of the Administrative Conference of the United States,) before the House Subcommittee on Commercial and Administrative Law, Committee on the Judiciary, 1 09th Cong., 2d Sess. (September 2007)(Reauthorization Hearing).

[87] *See, e.g. Regulatory Reform*, *supra* note 91, at 83; *Deossify Rulemaking, supra* note 91, at 65-66

[88] *See* Peter H Schuck & Donald Elliot, *To the Chevron Station: An Empirical Study of Federal Administrative Law*, 1990 Duke L. J. 984, 1022 (1990)(finding that during 1965,1974, 1984 and 1985, reviewing courts upheld only 43% of agency rules); Patricia M. Wald, *Judicial Review; Talking Points*, 48Admin L. Rev. 350 (1996) (noting that 36 major rules Reviewed by the District of Columbia Circuit during on year, 17 or 47% were remanded in part for reconsideration.) .

[89] Reauthorization Hearing, *supra* note 86 (Testimony of Professor Jody Freeman).

[90] *See, e.g.* Robert A. Anthony, *Interpretive Rules, Policy Statements, Guidances, Manuals, and the Like - Should Federal Agencies Use Them to Bind the Public?* 41 Duke L.J. 131 (1992); Robert A. Anthony, *"Well You Want the Permit, Don't You? ":Agency Efforts to Make Non-legislative Documents Bind the Public,* 44 Adm. L. Rev. 31 (1992); Michael Aismow, *California Undrground Regulations, 44 Adm. L. Rev 43 (1992).*

[91] *See, e.g.* Paul R. Verkuil, Comment, Rulemaking Ossification-A Modest Proposal, 47 Adm. L. Rev. 453(1995); Richard J. Pierce, Seven Ways to Deossify Agency Rulemaking, 47 Adm. L. Rev. 59, 71-93(1995). A more detailed discussion of the issues by court rulings on agency decisionmaking appears in this report's section of Judicial Review of Agency Rulemaking.

[92] Cynthia R. Farina, Undoing the New Deal Through the New Presidentialism, 22 Harv. J. Of L. & Pub. Policy, 227, 232, 235, 238 (1998).

[93] *Supra note* 86.

[94] A more detailed description of such process and a discussion of it's constructional basis appears in "*Whatever Happened to Congress Reviews of Agency Rulemaking? A Brief Overview, Assessment , and Proposal for Reform*," 51 Admin.L. Rev. 1051, 1083-1090 (1999).

[95] However, an appropriation to cover the costs of GAO's new assessment tasks is likely necessary.

[96] 462 US. 919 (1983).

[97] See, e.g., Changes in the OMB Regulatory Review Process by E.O. 13422, CRS Report RL33862 by Curtis W. Copeland, August 17, 2007; Rebecca Adams, Graham Leaves OIRA With a Full Job Jar, *CQ Week*, January 23, 2006; U.S. GAO. Rulemaking: OMB's Role in Reviews of Agencies' Draft Rules and the Transparency of Those Reviews, GAO-03-929 (September 2003; Stephen Power and Jacob M. Schlesinger, Redrawing the Lines: Bush's Rule Czar Brings Long Knife to New Regulations, *Wall St. Journal*, 6/12/02 at Al; Rebecca Adams, Regulating the Rulemakers: John Graham at OIRA, CQ Weekly, 2/23/02 at 520- 526.

[98] Seidenfeld, *supra* note 31, at 1090.

In: Revisiting and Evaluating the Congressional… ISBN: 978-1-60692-687-1
Editor: K. R. Williamson, pp. 59-82

Chapter 2

APPLICABILITY OF THE CONGRESSIONAL REVIEW ACT TO LETTER ON STATE CHILDREN'S HEALTH INSURANCE PROGRAM*

United States Government Accountability Office

B-316048

April 17, 2008

The Honorable
John D. Rockefeller, IV
Chairman
Subcommittee on Health Care
Committee on Finance
United States Senate

The Honorable
Olympia Snowe
Committee on Finance
United States Senate

* This is an edited, excerpted and augmented edition of a United States Government Accountability Office publication.

By letter of February 13, 2008, you asked whether an August 17, 2007 letter issued by the Centers for Medicare & Medicaid Services (CMS) to state health officials concerning the State Children's Health Insurance Program is a rule for the purpose of section 251 of the Contract with America Advancement Act of 1996,[1] commonly referred to as the Congressional Review Act (the Review Act). The Review Act is intended to keep Congress informed of the rulemaking activities of federal agencies and provides that before a rule can take effect, the agency must submit the rule to each House of Congress and the Comptroller General.[2] For the reasons discussed below and more fully explained in the enclosure, we conclude that the August 17, 2007 letter is a rule under the Review Act. Therefore, it must be submitted to Congress and the Comptroller General before it can take effect.

BACKGROUND

The State Children's Health Insurance Program (SCHIP) finances health care to low-income, uninsured children whose family incomes exceed the eligibility limits under their state's Medicaid program, but who cannot afford other health insurance coverage[3] To participate in SCHIP, a state must submit a plan that describes how its program meets applicable requirements and must receive approval of the plan from CMS.[4] States are required to amend their plans to reflect changes in federal law, regulation, or policy, and changes in the operation of their programs, including, for example, changes in eligibility criteria or benefits. [5]

As required by law, a state plan must describe the procedures used to ensure that coverage under the plan does not substitute for coverage under group health plans, generally referred to as "crowd out."[6] Regulations promulgated by CMS require states to adopt "reasonable procedures" to prevent crowd out.[7] Since CMS promulgated the regulations in 2001, states have adopted a number of different measures to prevent crowd out, which CMS has approved.

In its August 17 letter, CMS purports to clarify the statutory and regulatory requirements concerning prevention of crowd out for states wishing to provide SCHIP coverage to children with effective family incomes in excess of 250 percent of the federal poverty level (FPL) and identifies a number of particular measures that these states should adopt. The letter indicates that CMS will apply the measures to states' proposals to cover such children, as well as to states that already cover them. According to the letter, CMS may take corrective action against states that fail to adopt the identified measures within 12 months.

SUMMARY OF ANALYSIS

The definition of "rule" in the Review Act incorporates by reference the definition of "rule" in the Administrative Procedure Act (APA), with some exceptions. Our analysis of whether the August 17 letter is a rule under the Review Act thus entails determining whether the letter is a rule under the APA and whether it falls within any of the exceptions contained in the Review Act.[8] The APA definition of rule has been said to include "nearly every statement an agency may make."[9] It includes three elements that are relevant here: an agency statement is a rule if it is of general applicability; of future effect; and designed to implement, interpret, or prescribe law or policy.

On its face, the August 17 letter meets these criteria. The letter is of general, rather than particular, applicability since it extends to all states that seek to enroll children with effective family incomes exceeding 250 percent of the FPL in their SCHIP programs, as well as to all states that have already enrolled such children.[10] In addition, it is prospective in nature since it is concerned with policy considerations for the future rather than the evaluation of past or present conduct.[11] Finally, it purports to clarify and explain the manner in which CMS applies statutory and regulatory requirements to states that want to extend coverage under their SCHIP programs to children with effective family incomes above 250 percent of the FPL and seeks to promote the implementation of statutory requirements applicable to state plans. Accordingly, it is designed to implement, interpret, or prescribe law or policy.[12]

The history of the regulatory provision regarding substitution of coverage discussed in the letter lends support to our view that the letter is a rule. In the preamble to the proposed rule to implement SCHIP, CMS indicated that it could not require states to adopt any particular measures as part of the effort to prevent substitution of coverage, stating that it did not have a statutory or empirical basis for doing so.[13] CMS confirmed this interpretation in a final rule. [14] In its August 17 letter, however, CMS states that its experience and information derived from the operation of SCHIP programs have made it clear that the potential for substitution is greater at higher income levels, and states seeking to expand their SCHIP populations should implement specific strategies as "reasonable procedures" to prevent substitution of coverage (for example, a minimum 1-year period of uninsurance before receiving SCHIP coverage). Thus, the letter amounts to a marked departure from the agency's settled interpretation of the governing regulation, and case law indicates that such a change may be made only by a rule.[15] Moreover, the agency expressly relied on the letter to disapprove a request from the state of New York to amend its SCHIP plan to cover children with family incomes up to 400 percent of the FPL. The application of the letter to deny New York's proposed plan amendment only serves to confirm that the letter has binding effect and is, therefore, a rule.[16]

By letter of February 20, 2008, we requested the views of the General Counsel of the Department of Health and Human Services on whether the August 17 letter is a rule for purposes of the Review Act.[17] The response from the Director of the Center for Medicaid and State Operations within CMS did not directly address that issue. CMS indicated, however, that the letter is a "general statement of policy that announces the course which the agency intends to follow in adjudications concerning compliance with requirements already set forth in regulations."

As a conceptual matter, general statements of policy would appear to fit squarely within the definition of rule in the APA since they advise the public prospectively of the manner in which an agency proposes to exercise a discretionary power or what the agency will propose as policy,[18] and, in fact, courts have referred to them as rules.[19] While some cases seem to suggest that general statements of policy are not rules under the APA,[20] the better reading of these cases, in our opinion, is that statements of policy are not the type of rules for which the APA requires notice and comment procedures because they are tentative statements of future intent and by their nature do not have the force of law. Further, even if these cases are read to mean that general statements of policy are not rules under the APA, the August 17 letter does not have the characteristics of a general statement of policy identified in case law. Because the letter establishes a deadline by which "affected States" need to implement its measures or face the possibility of a corrective action by the agency, the letter evidences little, if any, of the tentativeness that is the hallmark of a policy statement.[21] Finally, as noted above, the agency has relied on the letter to disapprove a state plan amendment, treating the letter as if it were a binding rule.

CONCLUSION

The August 17 letter from CMS to state health officials is a statement of general applicability and future effect designed to implement, interpret, or prescribe law or policy with regard to SCHIP. Accordingly, it is a rule under the Congressional Review Act. Therefore, before it can take effect, it must be submitted to Congress and the Comptroller General.

If you have any questions concerning this opinion, please contact Dayna K. Shah, Managing Associate General Counsel, at (202) 512-8208; Helen T. Desaulniers,

Assistant General Counsel, at (202) 512-4740; or Kevin C. Milne, Deputy Assistant General Counsel, at (202) 512-4586.

Gary L. Kepplinger General Counsel
Enclosure
cc: James Stansel, Esq.
Acting General Counsel
Department of Health and Human Services

Janice Hoffman, Esq.
Associate General Counsel
Centers for Medicare & Medicaid Services Division
Department of Health and Human Services

Herb Kuhn
Acting Director
Center for Medicaid and State Operations
Centers for Medicare & Medicaid Services
Department of Health and Human Services

Jennifer Luong
Counselor on Oversight to the Assistant Secretary
Office of the Assistant Secretary for Legislation
Department of Health and Human Services

ENCLOSURE

The Centers for Medicare and Medicaid Services (CMS) issued a letter dated August 17, 2007 to certain state agencies concerning the State Children's Health Insurance Program. For the reasons discussed below, we conclude that the August 17 letter is a "rule" for the purpose of section 251 of the Contract with America Advancement Act of 1996,[22] commonly referred to as the Congressional Review Act (the Review Act). Therefore, in accordance with the Review Act, the letter must be submitted to Congress and the Comptroller General before it can take effect.

BACKGROUND

The State Children's Health Insurance Program

The State Children's Health Insurance Program (SCHIP), created in 1997, finances health care to low-income, uninsured children whose family incomes exceed the eligibility limits under their state's Medicaid program, but who cannot afford other health insurance coverage.[23] Like Medicaid, SCHIP is financed jointly by contributions from the federal government and the states. Under Medicaid, the federal government matches a portion of each state's Medicaid expenditures according to a matching rate that is based in part on the state's per capita income relative to the national average.[24] Under SCHIP, the federal government also matches a state's SCHIP expenditures, but at a rate that is generally higher than the Medicaid matching rate.[25]

To participate in SCHIP, a state must submit a state plan and must receive approval of the plan from CMS.[26] A state plan is a comprehensive written description of the operation of the state's SCHIP program, including eligibility standards and benefits provided, in sufficient detail for CMS to determine whether the plan meets applicable requirements.[27] The plan also assures CMS that the state will administer its program in accordance with those requirements.[28] Regulations require states to amend their state plans whenever necessary to reflect changes in federal law, regulations, policy interpretations, or court decisions, as well as changes in the operation of their programs, including, for example, changes in eligibility criteria or benefits.[29]

States have considerable flexibility under SCHIP in structuring their programs. They may expand their existing Medicaid programs to provide coverage to children who are eligible under SCHIP. Alternatively, they may implement separate child health programs. In addition, a state may have a combination of both a separate child health program and a Medicaid expansion.[30]

State SCHIP programs are subject to a number of statutory provisions that are designed to ensure that SCHIP coverage does not become a substitute for other public or private coverage. For example, section 2102(b)(3)(C) of the Social Security Act requires that a state plan include a description of the procedures used to ensure that state SCHIP coverage does not substitute for health insurance coverage under group health plans.[31] Under section 2102(c)(2) of the Social Security Act, states also must describe in their plans the procedures used to coordinate their SCHIP programs with other public and private programs.[32]

CMS has promulgated regulations designed to implement the statutory provisions to prevent substitution of coverage.[33] Among the regulations promulgated, section 457.805 of title 42, Code of Federal Regulations, requires that a state plan include a description of "reasonable procedures" to ensure that coverage provided under the state plan does not substitute for coverage provided under group health plans, referred to as "crowd out" provisions. Over time, states have proposed, and CMS has approved, a number of different measures to prevent substitution of coverage.

The August 17, 2007 Letter

On August 17, 2007, CMS issued a letter to state health officials (SHO #07-00 1) for the stated purpose of clarifying how CMS "applies existing statutory and regulatory requirements" for states that want to extend coverage under their SCHIP programs to children in families with effective family incomes above 250 percent of the federal poverty level (FPL). Specifically, the letter indicates that it is "clarifying that the reasonable procedures adopted by States to prevent crowd-out pursuant to 42 C.F.R. 457.805 should include . . . five general crowd-out strategies with certain important components." The five crowd out strategies identified in the letter are:

1 imposing waiting periods between dropping private coverage and enrollment in SCHIP;
2 imposing cost sharing in approximation to the cost of private coverage;
3 monitoring health insurance status at the time of application;
4 verifying family insurance status through insurance databases; and
5 preventing employers from changing dependent coverage policies that would favor a shift to public coverage.

In addition, the letter indicates that CMS "will expect" that these states incorporate the following components into their strategies to prevent substitution of coverage:

1 the cost sharing requirement under the state plan compared to the cost sharing required by competing private plans must not be more favorable to the public plan by more than 1 percent of the family income, unless the public plan's cost sharing is set at the 5 percent family cap;
2 the state must establish a minimum of a 1-year period of uninsurance for individuals prior to receiving coverage; and

3 monitoring and verification must include information regarding coverage provided by a noncustodial parent.

The letter also indicates that CMS will seek a number of assurances from states, including an assurance that the state has enrolled at least 95 percent of the children in the state with family incomes below 200 percent of the FPL who are eligible for SCHIP or Medicaid.

According to the August 17 letter, CMS will expect states that seek to amend their SCHIP state plans and section 1115 demonstrations[34] to cover children with effective family incomes above 250 percent of the FPL to include these specific measures. Furthermore, the letter indicates that CMS will apply the "review strategy" described in the letter to instances in which SCHIP plans and section 1115 programs already include these children. The letter indicates that states will be expected to amend their SCHIP plans or section 1115 demonstration programs in accordance with the provisions of the review strategy within 12 months or CMS "may pursue corrective action."

DISCUSSION

The Review Act is intended to keep Congress informed about the rulemaking activities of federal agencies and to allow for congressional review of rules.[35] The Review Act provides that before a rule can take effect, the agency promulgating the rule must submit to each House of Congress and the Comptroller General a report containing a copy of the rule; a concise general statement concerning the rule, including whether it is a major rule; and the proposed effective date of the rule.[36] Among other things, the Review Act sets forth a procedure for congressional disapproval of agency rules, specifically a joint resolution of disapproval effective upon signature by the President. The Review Act provides that no determination, finding, action, or omission under the Review Act shall be subject to judicial review.[37]

The definition of the term "rule" in the Review Act incorporates by reference the definition in the Administrative Procedure Act (APA), with some exceptions. Our analysis of whether the August 17 letter is a rule under the Review Act thus entails determining whether it is a rule under the APA and whether it falls within any of the exceptions contained in the Review Act.[38] The APA definition of rule has been said to include "nearly every statement an agency may make."[39] This definition is as follows:

> [T]he whole or a part of an agency statement of general or particular applicability and future effect designed to implement, interpret, or prescribe law or policy or describing the organization, procedure, or practice requirements of an agency and includes the approval or prescription for the future of rates, wages, corporate or financial structures or reorganizations thereof, prices, facilities, appliances, services or allowances therefor or of valuations, costs, or accounting, or practices bearing on any of the foregoing[40]

Agency statements that create binding legal norms--those that, for example, grant rights, impose obligations, or affect private interests--are rules under the APA.[41] These rules--usually called legislative rules--generally must be promulgated through notice and comment rulemaking procedures under 5 U.S.C. § 553. Courts have found that other agency pronouncements also are rules as defined in 5 U.S.C. § 551, even if they do not create binding legal norms and are not subject to notice and comment rulemaking requirements under section 553. For example, agency guidance documents and manuals have been held to be rules.[42] Agency documents that clarify or explain existing legal requirements also have been held to be rules.[43] Whether a particular agency pronouncement is a rule under section 551, therefore, does not turn on whether the rule is subject to notice and comment rulemaking requirements under section 553.

Legislative history of the Review Act confirms that the Review Act is intended to include within its purview almost all rules that an agency issues and is not limited to those rules that must be promulgated according to the notice and comment requirements in section 553 of the APA. In his floor statement during final consideration of the bill, Representative McIntosh, a principal sponsor of the legislation, pointed out that rules subject to congressional review are not just those rules subject to APA notice and comment requirements:

> Although agency interpretive rules, general statements of policy, guideline documents, and agency policy and procedure manuals may not be subject to the notice and comment provisions of section 553(c) of title 5, United States Code, these types of documents are covered under the congressional review provisions of the new chapter 8 of title 5.
>
> Under section 80 1(a), covered rules, with very few exceptions, may not go into effect until the relevant agency submits a copy of the rule and an accompanying report to both Houses of Congress. Interpretive rules, general statements of policy, and analogous agency policy guidelines are covered without qualification because they meet the definition of a 'rule' borrowed from section 551 of title 5, and are not excluded from the definition of a rule.[44]

Our prior opinions on the status of agency pronouncements under the Review Act reflect the breadth of the term "rule," applying a definition of the term that reaches pronouncements beyond those that require notice and comment rulemaking.[45]

The APA definition of rule includes three elements relevant to our consideration of whether the August 17 letter is a rule: an agency statement is a rule if it is of general applicability; of future effect; and designed to implement, interpret, or prescribe law or policy. An examination of the text of the letter itself indicates that it meets these criteria. The letter is of general, rather than particular, applicability since it extends to all states that seek to enroll children with effective family incomes exceeding 250 percent of the FPL in their SCHIP programs, as well as to all states that have already enrolled such children.[46] In addition, it is of future effect since it concerns policy considerations for the future rather than the evaluation of past and present conduct.[47] Further, by its own terms, the letter purports to clarify and explain statutory and regulatory requirements. The very first sentence explains that the letter "clarifies how [CMS] applies existing statutory and regulatory requirements" with regard to requests from states to extend coverage under SCHIP to children with effective family incomes above 250 percent of the FPL. The letter also purports to explain the requirements under 42 C.F.R. § 457.805 regarding state efforts to prevent substitution of coverage and the measures that states seeking to cover these populations should take to prevent substitution of coverage. In addition, the letter indicates that the requested assurances help ensure the coordination of SCHIP coverage with other coverage, thus indicating that the assurances promote the implementation of one of the statutory objectives for state plans.[48] In particular, it indicates that states that already have included coverage under their SCHIP programs for children with effective family incomes above 250 percent of the FPL are expected to adjust their state plans accordingly. Because the letter purports to provide an explanation of statutory and regulatory requirements and to explain how the provisions adopted effectuate both legal requirements and policy choices attendant to administration of SCHIP, the document on its face is designed to implement, interpret, or prescribe law or policy within the meaning of section 55 1(4) of the APA.

The history of 42 C.F.R. § 457.805, the regulation that the August 17 letter purports to clarify, supports our view that the letter is a rule. In the preamble to the proposed rule to implement SCHIP, CMS considered whether to require states to adopt a set of particular measures to prevent substitution of coverage and expressly declined to impose such a requirement. CMS concluded that, based on its interpretation of the governing statute and evidence, it did not have a basis upon which to require such measures. CMS explained its position as follows:

> The other option that we considered was to require a set of specific procedures that each State would have to use to address substitution [of coverage]. We rejected this option because the statute authorizes States to design approaches to prevent substitution, not the Federal government. We also recognized that there is not substantial evidence favoring any specific approach to reduce the potential for substitution.[49]

CMS confirmed this interpretation in a final rule.[50] The August 17 letter, however, explains that CMS's experience and information derived from the operation of SCHIP programs have made it clear that the potential for substitution is greater at higher income levels. The letter further states that CMS will expect states to undertake five specific measures, include three components as part of those measures, and make three additional assurances in order to cover children with effective family incomes above 250 percent of the FPL under SCHIP. In this respect, the letter amounts to a marked departure from the agency's interpretation of the regulation regarding substitution of coverage in the preambles to the proposed and final rules. Accordingly, because of this new regulatory interpretation and because an agency may only change a settled interpretation of its own rules through the promulgation of an amending rule, the letter serves the same purpose as a rule.[51]

CMS's application of the August 17 letter only serves to confirm that the letter has binding effect and is, therefore, a rule. In April 2007, the state of New York requested permission from CMS to amend its SCHIP plan to provide coverage to children with family incomes up to 400 percent of the FPL. CMS expressly relied on the August 17 letter to deny the request. In a letter dated September 7, 2007 to the state of New York, CMS stated, in part, the following:

> New York has not demonstrated that its program operates in an effective and efficient manner with respect to the core population of targeted low-income children. Specifically, it has failed to provide assurances that the State has enrolled at least 95 percent of the children in the core targeted low-income child population, those with family incomes below 200 percent of the FPL. As outlined in an August 17, 2007, letter to State Health Officials, such assurances are necessary to ensure that expansion to higher income populations does not interfere with the effective and efficient provision of child health assistance.

In explaining the applicable requirements under 42 C.F.R. § 457.805, CMS went on to state additional grounds for its denial of New York's request to amend its SCHIP plan:

> At the high proposed family income eligibility levels, reasonable procedures [to prevent substitution of coverage] should include a full range

> of procedures to discourage substitution. New York's proposal does not include procedures to prevent such substitution that include a 1-year period of uninsurance for populations over 250 percent of the FPL. Additionally, New York's proposed cost sharing has not met the requirement that cost sharing under the State plan compared to cost sharing required by competing private plans not be more favorable to the public plan by more than 1 percent of the family income, nor has the State proposed to set its cost sharing at the 5 percent family cap. . . .
>
> For these reasons . . . I am unable to approve this [State Plan Amendment] for expanding coverage. This disapproval is consistent with the August 17, 2007 letter to State Health Officials discussing how these existing statutory and regulatory requirements should be applied to all States expanding SCHIP effective eligibility levels above 250 percent of the FPL.

CMS's action demonstrates that the letter represents the agency's decision to bind itself to the application of the letter's terms and to give the letter present and binding effect.[52]

By letter of February 20, 2008, we requested the views of the General Counsel of the Department of Health and Human Services (HHS) on whether the August 17 letter is a rule for purposes of the Review Act.[53] The written response from the Director of the Center for Medicaid and State Operations within CMS did not address this issue. The response stated that it would be inappropriate to address legal issues related to the August 17 letter because the letter is the subject of a number of lawsuits.[54] Nevertheless, CMS indicated that the August 17 letter is a "general statement of policy that announces the course which the agency intends to follow in adjudications concerning compliance with requirements already set forth in regulations." The agency also referred us to a document prepared by the Department of Justice, which asserted that the August 17 letter was a general statement of policy.

The agency's characterization of the August 17 letter as a general statement of policy raises one issue relevant to our consideration: whether a general statement of policy is a rule under section 55 1(4) of the APA.[55] The term "general statements of policy" is not defined in the APA or in its legislative history. The Attorney General's Manual on the Administrative Procedure Act, which the United States Supreme Court has frequently referred to as an authoritative source for interpreting provisions of the APA,[56] defines the term as "statements issued by an agency to advise the public prospectively of the manner in which the agency proposes to exercise a discretionary power."[57] A statement of policy, therefore, as the U.S. Court of Appeals for the District of Columbia Circuit has stated, announces the agency's tentative intentions for the future, and "what the agency seeks to establish as policy."[58] In this way, the general statement of policy serves a number of useful functions, including the facilitation of long range planning within the regulated industry and the promotion of uniformity in areas of national concern.[59]

Section 55 1(4) includes within the meaning of rule a statement of general or particular applicability and future effect designed to implement, interpret, or prescribe law or policy. As a device that provides information on the manner in which an agency will exercise its authority or what the agency will seek to propose as policy, a general statement of policy would appear to fit squarely within this category. Further, in discussing policy statements under the APA, courts have referred to them as rules.[60]

Nevertheless, some court decisions seem to suggest that general statements of policy are not rules under the APA, which would raise, of course, the question whether they are rules under the Review Act.[61] The holdings of these cases did not address whether the agency pronouncements were rules for the purpose of section 551, but, instead, whether they were rules that should have been promulgated according to notice and comment rulemaking requirements under section 553 or whether they were subject to review. The better reading of these cases, in our opinion, is not that general statements of policy are not rules under 551, but that statements of policy are not legislative rules because they are tentative statements of future intent and by their nature do not have the force of law.

Even if general statements of policy are not rules for purposes of section 551, however, the August 17 letter does not qualify as a general statement of policy. In determining whether a particular agency pronouncement is a general statement of policy, courts begin with the language of the document itself and the agency's own characterization of the pronouncement.[62] Although courts give deference to an agency's characterization, the label that an agency puts on the exercise of its administrative power is not conclusive[63] In general, if the language of the pronouncement indicates that the agency's views are tentative or simply a guide as to how the agency may exercise its authority, and the agency in fact does not treat the statement as a binding norm, then the document may be a policy statement. If, however, the document, either by its terms or as applied by the agency, imposes requirements or obligations, it would not be considered a general statement of policy.

One case in particular, cited by the Department of Justice in the memorandum included in CMS's response to our request for the agency's views, provides a useful explanation of the type of language typically found in an agency general statement of policy. In Pacific Gas and Electric Co. v. Federal Power Commission,[64] the United States Court of Appeals for the District of Columbia Circuit determined that a Federal Power Commission pronouncement was a general statement of policy exempt from notice and comment rulemaking requirements. The pronouncement, styled a "statement of policy," expressed the Commission's view of how deliveries of natural gas should be prioritized during periods of shortage. The pronouncement stated that the Commission intended to follow this priority schedule unless a particular pipeline company demonstrated that a different curtailment plan (governing allocation of available supply among customers) better served the public interest. After the statement was issued, a number of parties objected to the Commission's statement, most of whom were the natural gas customers that had been assigned a low priority under the priority schedule. Among their objections was the claim that the statement was in effect a substantive rule, and not a statement of policy.

In reaching its conclusion that the statement was indeed a statement of policy, the court noted the tentative nature of the statement, as well as the Commission's acknowledgment that any particular decisions on curtailment could only be made in further proceedings. Specifically, the court found it significant that the statement indicated it was the curtailment policy that the Commission "proposes to implement" and the "plan preferred by the Commission," which "will serve as a guide in other proceedings." The Commission itself intended the statement only "to state initial guidelines as a means of facilitating curtailment planning and the adjudication of curtailment cases." In addition, the statement also indicated that, although it informed the public of the types of plans the Commission might approve, there was no assurance that any such plan would be approved. Finally, the court noted that the statement indicated that during subsequent proceedings to determine particular curtailments, affected parties would have an opportunity not only to challenge the merits of the proposed plan, but to demonstrate that the plan was inappropriate in particular circumstances. In effect, the Commission statement was a starting point to frame consideration of future proposals.

If we analyze CMS's August 17 letter using the criteria used by the court to determine that the Commission's pronouncement was simply a statement of policy, we conclude that the letter does not meet the criteria. The August 17 letter evidences little, if any, language of tentativeness or inconclusiveness. The specific measures are not characterized as "proposals" or measures that are under development or to be implemented or adopted by later action. On the contrary, the letter sets forth specific strategies that states seeking to expand their SCRIP populations should implement as "reasonable procedures" to prevent substitution of coverage. While states previously identified and adopted one or more of the specified strategies, the August 17 letter indicates that all of them should be included as "reasonable procedures." There is no indication that the strategies are only guidelines that may or may not be applied in subsequent proceedings. In addition, the letter contains no express mention that exceptions will be considered in particular instances. Finally, the time frame specified in the letter for states to conform to the CMS "review strategy" evidences the agency's intention to give the letter present and binding effect:

> CMS will apply this review strategy to SCRIP state plans and section 1115 demonstration waivers that include SCRIP populations, and will work with States that currently provide services to children with effective family incomes over 250 percent of FPL. We expect affected States to amend their SCRIP state plan (or 1115 demonstration) in accordance with this review strategy within 12 months, or CMS may pursue corrective action.

If the letter were simply precatory or tentative in nature, then there would be no need to establish a deadline by which states would need to implement the measures in the letter or face the possibility of a corrective action by the agency.[65] The inference to be drawn from the letter, therefore, is that states that do not conform to or adopt the measures described in the letter will likely be found to be not in compliance with SCRIP requirements.

In addition to the particular language of a statement, courts look to an agency's actions in relation to the statement to determine whether it is a general statement of policy. As a number of courts have noted, a critical test of whether a rule is a general statement of policy is its practical effect in a subsequent administrative proceeding. In subsequent proceedings, if the agency relies solely on the pronouncement itself to determine rights and obligations of others, the agency has treated the policy statement as if it were a binding rule, not a general statement of policy.[66] As we explained above, CMS's express reliance on the August 17 letter to deny the state of New York's request to amend its SCHIP plan leads us to conclude that the letter is not a policy statement. Our conclusion that the August 17 letter is not a general statement of policy is reinforced by our observation that it reflects a significant change in the agency's settled interpretation of 42 C.F.R. § 457.805, which policy statements by their nature do not do.[67]

CONCLUSION

Based on our analysis of the August 17, 2007 letter to state health officials, it is our opinion that the letter is a rule for the purpose of the Review Act. The letter, as discussed above, is a statement of general applicability and future effect designed to implement, interpret, or prescribe law or policy with regard to the SCHIP program. Furthermore, we do not believe that the August 17 letter comes within any of the exceptions to the definition of rule contained in the Review Act.

We express no opinion on the applicability of any other legal requirements, including, but not limited to, notice and comment rulemaking requirements under the

APA, or whether the August 17 letter would be a valid interpretation of statutes or regulations. As a legal matter, the resolution of such issues is not necessary to our determination whether the August 17 letter is a rule for purposes of the Review Act.

Accordingly, given our conclusions above, and in accordance with the provisions of 5 U.S.C. § 801(a)(1), the letter must be submitted to Congress and the Comptroller General before it can take effect.

REFERENCES

[1] Pub. L. No. 104-121, § 251, 110 Stat. 847, 868-74, codifed at 5 U.S.C. §§ 801-808.

[2] 5 U.S.C. § 801(a)(1).

[3] See 42 U.S.C. § 1397aa.

[4] 42 U.S.C. § 1397aa(b). The authority vested in the Secretary of Health and Human Services to approve and disapprove SCHIP state plans and plan amendments has been delegated to the Administrator of CMS. Sate Chd Health; Impementing Reguations for the Sate Chdren's Healthnsurance Program, 64 Fed. Reg. 60882, 60895 (Nov. 8, 1999) (proposed rule).

[5] 42 C.F.R. § 457.60.

[6] 42 U.S.C. § 1397bb(b)(3)(C).

[7] 42 C.F.R. § 457.805.

[8] The Review Act excepts the following from its definition of rule: (1) rules of particular applicability, including a rule that approves or prescribes for future application rates, wages, prices, services, or allowances therefor, corporate or financial structures, reorganizations, mergers, or acquisitions thereof, or accounting practices or disclosures bearing on any of the foregoing; (2) rules relating to agency management or personnel; and (3) rules of agency organization, procedure, or practice that do not substantially affect the rights or obligations of non-agency parties. 5 U.S.C. § 804(3). As discussed below, the letter is not a statement of particular applicability; rather, it substantially affects all states that seek to cover children with effective family incomes in excess of 250 percent of the FPL, as well as those states that already cover these children. The letter does not relate to agency management or personnel, and it does not relate to "agency organization, procedure, or practice" with no substantial effect on non-

agency parties. Accordingly, we do not believe that any of these three exceptions applies to the August 17 letter.

[9] Baterton v. Marshall, 648 F.2d 694, 700 (D.C. Cir. 1980) (citing 5 U.S.C. § 551(4)). Section 551(4) of title 5, United States Code, defines the term "rule" in relevant part as "[t]he whole or a part of an agency statement of general or particular applicability and future effect designed to implement, interpret, or prescribe law or policy or describing the organization, procedure, or practice requirements of an agency . . ."

[10] Cf. U.S. Dep't of Justice Attorney General's Manual on the Adminstrave Procedure Act 13 (1947) (the term "rule" includes statements of particular applicability applying either to a class or to a single person).

[11] See Bowen v. GeorgetownUnversity Hospal, 488 U.S. 204, 216 (1988) (Scalia, J., concurring) ("future effect" means that agency statement will have legal consequences for the future); see also U.S. Dep't of Justice Attorney General's Manual on the Admnistrave Procedure Act at 14 (rulemaking regulates the future conduct of either groups of persons or a single person and is essentially legislative in nature because it operates in the future and is primarily concerned with policy considerations, while adjudication is concerned with the determination of past and present rights and liabilities).

[12] See A.D. Transport Express, Inc. v. Uned States, 290 F.3d 761, 768 (6th Cir. 2002) (order explaining agency regulation is an interpretative rule under the APA); Guardian Federal Savings and Loan Ass'n vFederal Savngs and Loan Insurance Corp., 589 F.2d 658, 664 (D.C. Cir. 1978) (agency statements that clarify laws or regulations are rules under the APA).

[13] 64 Fed. Reg. at 60921-22.

[14] See Sate Chd Health; Implementing Reguations for the State Chdren's Health Insurance Program 66 Fed. Reg. 2490, 2601-05 (Jan. 11, 2001) (final rule).

[15] See SBC Inc. v. Federal Communications Commission, 414 F.3d 486, 498 (3d Cir. 2005) (if agency's present interpretation of regulation is a fundamental modification of previous interpretation, the modification can only be accomplished through notice and comment rulemaking); Shell Offshore Incv. Babbit, 238 F.3d 622, 629 (5th Cir. 2001) (settled policy of an agency is binding on the agency and may be changed only through a rule); Alaska Professiona Hunters Ass'n v. Federal Aviation Admnistraon, 177 F.3d 1030, 1033-34 (D.C. Cir. 1999) (an agency is bound by settled interpretation given to its own regulation that agency can change only by rulemaking).

[16] See Appaachan Power Co. v. Environmental Proection Agency, 208 F.3d 1015, 1020-21 (D.C. Cir. 2000) (if an agency treats a pronouncement as if it were controlling, if it bases enforcement actions on the policies in the document, and if it leads private parties or states to believe it must comply with the pronouncement's terms, it is a substantive rule, not a general statement of policy); Guardan FederaSavngs and Loan Ass'n, 589 F.2d at 666 (in subsequent administrative proceeding, agency cannot claim that prior statement of policy itself resolves contested issues).

[17] In documents filed in related litigation, the Department of Justice has characterized the August 17 letter as a rule. See New York v. United States Dep't of Health and Human Services, No. 07 Civ. 08621 (S.D.N.Y. filed Oct. 4, 2007) (Def's Mem. Supp. Mot. Dismiss, p. 33).

[18] See U.S. Dep't of Justice Atorney General's Manual on the Administrave Procedure Act at 30, n.3.

[19] See, e.g., Chrysler v. Brown, 441 U.S. 281, 301 (1979) ("the central distinction among agency regulations found in the APA is that between 'substantive rules' on the one hand and 'interpretive rules, general statements of policy, or rules of agency organization, procedure, or practice' on the other"); Noel v. Chapman, 508 F.2d 1023, 1030 (2d Cir. 1975) (general statement of policy is a rule directed at agency staff on how it will perform discretionary function); Guardian Federal Savngs and Loan Assn, 589 F.2d at 666 (describing test for determining whether "a rule is a general statement of policy").

[20] See, e.g., Sugar Cane Growers Cooperative o Florda v. Veneman, 289 F.3d 89, 95 (D.C. Cir. 2002) (some agency pronouncements lack the firmness of a prescribed standard to be considered rules); Syncor Inernational Corp. v. Shalala, 127 F.3d 90, 94 (D.C. Cir. 1997) (the primary distinction between a rule and a general statement of policy is whether the agency intends to bind itself to a legal position); Pacific Gas and Electric Co. v. Federa Power Commission, 506 F.2d 33, 37 (D.C. Cir. 1974) (suggesting that policy statements are not rules under the APA).

[21] See Pacific Gas and Eectrc Co., 506 F.2d at 36-45 (discussing the language of a "statement of policy" and noting that such a statement announces tentative intentions for the future); c. CommunityNutrition Institute v Young, 818 F.2d 943, 947 (D.C. Cir. 1987) (agency prescribed standard from which regulated entities could obtain "exception" or risk enforcement action indicated standard was binding).

[22] Pub. L. No. 104-121, § 251, 110 Stat. 847, 868-74, codifed at 5 U.S.C. §§ 801-808.

[23] See 42 U.S.C. § 1397aa. Medicaid finances health care for certain low-income families, children, pregnant women, elderly persons, and persons with disabilities. In general, under SCHIP, a state is allowed to cover children in families with incomes up to 200 percent of the federal poverty level or 50 percentage points above the state's Medicaid income eligibility limit as of March 31, 1997. See 42 U.S.C. §§1397jj(b)(1) and (c)(4).

[24] 42 U.S.C. §§ 1396b(a), 1396d(b).

[25] See 42 U.S.C. § 1397ee(a).

[26] 42 U.S.C. § 1397aa(b). The authority vested in the Secretary of Health and Human Services to approve and disapprove SCHIP state plans and plan amendments has been delegated to the Administrator of CMS. Sate Chd Health; Impementing Reguations for the Sate Chdren's Healthnsurance Program, 64 Fed. Reg. 60882, 60895 (Nov. 8, 1999) (proposed rule).

[27] 42 C.F.R. § 457.50.

[28] Id.

[29] 42 C.F.R. § 457.60.

[30] 42 U.S.C. § 1397aa(a); 42 C.F.R. § 457.70.

[31] 42 U.S.C. § 1397bb(b)(3)(C). CMS explained in the preamble to a final rule implementing SCHIP that the potential for substitution of SCHIP coverage for private coverage exists because SCHIP coverage may be less expensive than private coverage or provide better coverage than some individuals or employers could purchase with their own funds. See State Child Health; Impementing Reguations forthe Sate Chdrens Health Insurance Program, 66 Fed. Reg. 2490, 2602 (Jan. 11, 2001) (final rule).

[32] 42 U.S.C. § 1397bb(c)(2).

[33] See 64 Fed. Reg. at 60921-23; 66 Fed. Reg. at 2601-2610.

[34] Section 1115 of the Social Security Act authorizes the Secretary of Health and Human Services to conduct demonstration programs likely to assist in promoting the objectives of specified programs. 42 U.S.C. § 1315; 42 U.S.C. § 1397gg(e).

[35] See 142 Cong. Rec. H3005 (daily ed. Mar. 28, 1996) (statement of Rep. McIntosh); see also New York v. American Eectrc Power Service Corp., Nos. 2:04 CV 1098, 2:05 CV 360, 2006 WL 1331543, at *13 (S.D. Ohio Mar. 21, 2006); United States v. Southern Indiana Gas and Elecric Co., No. IP99-1692-C-M/S, 2002 WL 31427523, at *3 (S.D. Ind. Oct. 24, 2002); Texas Savngs & Community Bankers Ass'n v Federal Housing Fnance Board, No. A 97 CA 421 SS, 1998 WL 842181, at *7 (W.D. Tex. June 25, 1998).

[36] 5 U.S.C. § 801(a)(1). On the date the report is submitted, the agency also must submit to the Comptroller General and make available to each House of Congress certain other documents, including a cost-benefit analysis, if any, and agency actions relevant to the Regulatory Flexibility Act and the Unfunded Mandates Reform Act of 1995, and any other relevant information or requirements under any other legislation or any relevant executive orders. 5 U.S.C. § 801(a)(1)(B)(i)-(iv). For rules that federal agencies identify as major rules, the Comptroller General is required under the Review Act to provide a report to the committees of jurisdiction in each House on whether the agency complied with certain procedural requirements. 5 U.S.C. § 801(a)(2)(A).

[37] 5 U.S.C. § 805. A number of federal courts have concluded that an agency's failure to submit a rule in accordance with the Review Act is not reviewable. See Amercan Electric Power Servce Corp., 2006 WL 1331543, at *13; UnedStates v. Amercan Eectrc Power Servce Corp., 218 F. Supp. 2d 931, 949 (S.D. Ohio 2002); Texas Savings & Community Bankers Ass'n, 1998 WL 842181, at *7. One court has ruled that the Review Act does not preclude review of the agency's failure to submit a rule as required by the Review Act. See Southern Indiana Gas and Electric Co., 2002 WL 31427523, at *5–*6.

[38] The Review Act excepts the following from its definition of rule: (1) rules of particular applicability, including a rule that approves or prescribes for future application rates, wages, prices, services, or allowances therefor, corporate or financial structures, reorganizations, mergers, or acquisitions thereof, or accounting practices or disclosures bearing on any of the foregoing; (2) rules relating to agency management or personnel; and (3) rules of agency organization, procedure, or practice that do not substantially affect the rights or obligations of non-agency parties. 5 U.S.C. § 804(3). As discussed below, the letter is not a statement of particular applicability; rather, it substantially affects all states that seek to cover children with effective family incomes in excess of 250 percent of the FPL, as well as those states that already cover these children. The letter does not relate to agency management or personnel, and it does not relate to "agency organization, procedure, or practice" with no substantial affect on non-agency parties. Accordingly, we do not believe that any of these three exceptions applies to the August 17 letter.

[39] Baterton v. Marshall, 648 F.2d 694, 700 (D.C. Cir. 1980).

[40] 5 U.S.C. § 551(4).

[41] Batterton, 648 F.2d at 700-02.

[42] See Reno v. Koray, 515 U.S. 50, 60–61 (1995) (internal agency guideline was a rule under the APA); Shalala v. Guernsey Memoral Hospal, 514 U.S. 87, 99–100 (1995) (provision of the Medicare Provider Reimbursement Manual was a rule under the APA); Appaachan Power Co. v. EnvironmentalProtection Agency, 208 F.3d 1015, 1021–22 (D.C. Cir. 2000) (agency guidance document can be rule under the APA); Professionals and Paents for Customized Care v Shalala, 56 F.3d 592, 601–02 (5th Cir. 1995) (FDA Compliance Policy Guide was a rule, but was exempt from notice and comment procedures as a statement of policy or interpretative rule).

[43] See, e.g., AD. Transport Express, Inc. v. Unted States, 290 F.3d 761, 768 (6th Cir. 2002) (order explaining agency regulation is an interpretative rule under the APA); Guardian Federal Savings and Loan Assn v. Federal Savngs and Loan Insurance Corp., 589 F.2d 658, 664 (D.C. Cir. 1978) (agency statements that clarify laws or regulations are rules under the APA).

[44] 142 Cong. Rec. H3005 (daily ed. Mar. 28, 1996) (statement of Rep. McIntosh).

[45] See, e.g., B-287557, May 14, 2001 ("record of decision" issued by the Fish and Wildlife Service of the Department of Interior in connection with a federal irrigation project was a rule); B-274505, September 16, 1996 (memorandum issued by Secretary of Agriculture in connection with the Emergency Salvage Timber Sale Program was a rule).

[46] Cf. U.S. Dep't of Justice, Atorney General's Manual on the Administrative Procedure Act 13 (1947) (the term "rule" includes statements of particular applicability applying either to a class or to a single person).

[47] See Bowen v. GeorgetownUnversity Hospal, 488 U.S. 204, 216 (1988) (Scalia, J., concurring) ("future effect" means that statement will have legal consequences for the future); see also U.S Dep't of Justice, Atorney General's Manual on the Administrative Procedure Act at 13-14 (rulemaking regulates the future conduct of either groups of persons or a single person and is essentially legislative in nature because it operates in the future and is primarily concerned with policy considerations, while adjudication is concerned with the determination of past and present rights and liabilities.)

[48] Among the statutory provisions that the letter expressly refers to is section 2101(a) of the Social Security Act, which provides, in pertinent part: Purpose.–The purpose of this title [XXI] is to provide funds to States to enable them to initiate and expand the provision of child health assistance to uninsured, low-income children in an effective and efficient manner that is

coordinated with other sources of health benefits coverage for children. 42 U.S.C. § 1397aa(a).

[49] 64 Fed. Reg. at 60921-22.

[50] See 66 Fed. Reg. at 2601-05.

[51] See SBI Inc v Federal Communicaions Commission, 414 F.3d 486, 498 (3d Cir. 2005) (if an agency's present interpretation of a regulation is a fundamental modification of a previous interpretation, the modification must be accomplished through notice and comment rulemaking); Shel Offshore Inc. v. Babbitt, 238 F.3d 622, 629 (5th Cir. 2001) (a settled policy of an agency is binding on the agency and may be changed only through a rule); Alaska Professiona Hunters Ass'n v. Federal Aviation Admnistraon, 177 F.3d 1030, 1033-34 (D.C. Cir. 1999) (an agency is bound by settled interpretation given to its own regulation that the agency can change only by rulemaking).

[52] See Appalachian Power Co., 208 F.3d at 1020-21 (if an agency treats a pronouncement as if it were controlling, if it bases enforcement actions on the policies in the document, and if it leads private parties or states to believe it must comply with the pronouncement's terms, it is a rule); Public Citizen, Inc. v. Unted States Nuclear Reguatory Commission, 940 F.2d 679, 682 (D.C. Cir. 1991) (where language and context of a statement are inconclusive, court will turn to agency's actual application to determine nature of agency pronouncement); McLouth Steel Producs Corp. v. Thomas, 838 F.2d 1317, 1321 (D.C. Cir. 1988) (because agency used policy statement to determine regulated entities' obligations, policy statement is, therefore, a rule); Guardian Federal Savngs and Loan Ass'n, 589 F.2d at 666 (form of a regulation is not controlling; substance and effect will determine whether agency statement is a rule).

[53] See GAO, Procedures and Pracices for Legal Decsions and Opinions, GAO-06-1064SP (Washington, D.C.: Sept. 2006), avaiabe at www.gao.gov/legal/resources.html.

[54] In documents filed in litigation, the Department of Justice has characterized the letter as an interpretative rule. See New York v. Unted States Dept o Health and Human Services, No. 07 Civ. 08621 (S.D.N.Y. filed Oct. 4, 2007) (Def's Mem. Supp. Mot. Dismiss, p. 33). i ' f

[55] "General statements of policy" are expressly excepted from notice and comment rulemaking requirements under section 553 of the APA. In court filings submitted by the Department of Justice in separate litigation, HHS contends that the August 17 letter is not subject to notice and comment rulemaking requirements.

[56] See, e.g., Guernsey Memoral Hospal, 514 U.S. at 99; Georgetown Unversity Hospital, 488 U.S. at 218.

[57] U.S. Dep't of Justice Attorney General's Manual on the Adminstrave Procedure Act at 14.

[58] See Pacific Gas and Eectrc Co. v. Federa Power Commssion, 506 F.2d 33, 38 (D.C. Cir. 1974).

[59] Id.

[60] See, e.g., Chrysler v. Brown, 441 U.S. 281, 315 (1979) ("the central distinction among agency regulations found in the APA is that between 'substantive rules' on the one hand and 'interpretive rules, general statements of policy, or rules of agency organization, procedure, or practice' on the other"); Professionals and Paens for Customized Care, 56 F.3d at 596 (discussing whether policy statement at issue is interpretative rule or legislative rule); Noel v. Chapman, 508 F.2d 1023, 1030 (2d Cir. 1975) (general statement of policy is a rule directed at agency staff on how it will perform discretionary function); Guardian Federal Savngs and Loan Ass'n, 589 F.2d at 666 (describing test for determining whether "a rule is a general statement of policy").

[61] See, e.g., Sugar Cane Growers Cooperative o Florda v. Veneman, 289 F.3d 89, 95 (D.C. Cir. 2002) (some agency pronouncements lack the firmness of a prescribed standard to be considered rules); Syncor Inernational Corp. v. Shalala, 127 F.3d 90, 94 (D.C. Cir. 1997) (the primary distinction between a rule and a general statement of policy is whether the agency intends to bind itself to a legal position); Pacific Gas and Electric Co., 506 F.2d at 37 (suggesting that policy statements are not rules under the APA).

[62] Professionals and Patiens for Customized Care, 56 F.3d at 596.

[63] See id. (what the agency in fact does in relation to an agency statement is dispositive); Uned Sates Gypsum Co. v. Muszynski, 209 F. Supp. 2d 308, 309–10 (S.D.N.Y. 2002) (an advisory memorandum that was applied by agency as a rule was a rule).

[64] 506 F.2d 33 (D.C. Cir. 1974).

[65] Cf. Community Nutrition Institute v. Young, 818 F.2d 943, 947 (D.C. Cir. 1987) (agency prescribed standard from which regulated entities could obtain "exception" or risk enforcement action indicated standard was binding).

[66] See Public Citizen, Inc., 940 F.2d at 682-83 (courts look to agency's actual application of statement to determine its nature if language and context of agency statement are not conclusive); Guardan Federal Savngs and Loan

Ass'n, 589 F.2d at 666 (in subsequent administrative proceeding, agency cannot claim that prior statement of policy itself resolves contested issues).

[67] See Syncor International Corp., 127 F.3d at 94 (a general statement of policy does not impose, elaborate, or interpret a legal norm, but explains the agency's manner of enforcing the existing legal norm).

In: Revisiting and Evaluating the Congressional... ISBN: 978-1-60692-687-1
Editor: K. R. Williamson, pp. 83-93

Chapter 3

CONGRESSIONAL REVIEW ACT: APPLICABILITY TO CMS LETTER ON STATE CHILDREN'S HEALTH INSURANCE PROGRAM*

Dayna K. Shah

WHAT GAO FOUND

The definition of "rule" in the Congressional Review Act incorporates by reference the definition of "rule" in the Administrative Procedure Act (APA), with some exceptions. The APA definition of rule includes three elements relevant to GAO's consideration of the SCHIP letter: an agency statement is a rule if it is of general applicability; of future effect; and designed to implement, interpret, or prescribe law or policy. GAO concluded that the letter meets these criteria and that none of the exceptions in the Review Act apply. GAO found the letter to be of general applicability since it extends to all states that seek to enroll children with effective family incomes exceeding 250 percent of the FPL in their SCHIP programs, as well as to states that have already enrolled such children. In addition, GAO found it to be of future effect, that is, concerned with policy considerations for the future rather than the evaluation of past or present conduct. Finally, GAO found that the letter is designed to implement, interpret, or prescribe law or policy since it purports to clarify and explain the manner in which CMS applies statutory and regulatory requirements to states that want to extend

* This is an edited, excerpted and augmented edition of a United States Government Accountability Office publication, Report GAO-08-785T, dated May 15, 2008.

coverage under their SCHIP programs to children with effective family incomes above 250 percent of the FPL and seeks to promote the implementation of statutory requirements applicable to state plans.

The history of the regulatory provision regarding substitution of coverage supported the view that the August 17 letter is a rule. In issuing the proposed and final rules to implement SCHIP, CMS indicated that it could not require states to adopt any particular measures to prevent substitution of coverage, stating that it did not have a statutory or empirical basis for doing so. In its August 17 letter, however, CMS states that its experience and information derived from the operation of SCHIP programs have made it clear that the potential for substitution is greater at higher income levels, and states seeking to expand their SCHIP populations should implement specific strategies to prevent substitution of coverage. Thus, the letter amounts to a marked departure from the agency's settled interpretation of the regulation regarding substitution of coverage, and case law indicates that such a change may be made only by rule. Moreover, the agency expressly relied on the letter to disapprove a state request to amend its SCHIP plan to cover children with family incomes in excess of 250 percent of the FPL, confirming that the letter has binding effect and is, therefore, a rule.

In response to GAO's inquiries, CMS stated that the letter is a general statement of policy announcing the course that the agency intends to follow in adjudications concerning compliance with requirements already set forth in regulations. The GAO opinion explained that statements of policy would appear to fit within the definition of rule in the APA and that courts have referred to them as rules. However, GAO also concluded that the August 17 letter does not have the characteristics of a statement of policy identified in case law. It evidences little, if any, of the tentativeness that is the hallmark of a policy statement, and the agency has relied on the letter to disapprove a state plan amendment, treating the letter as if it were a binding rule.

WHY GAO DID THIS STUDY

The State Children's Health Insurance Program (SCHIP) finances health care to low-income, uninsured children whose family incomes exceed the eligibility limits under their state's Medicaid program, but who cannot afford other health insurance coverage. To participate in SCHIP, a state must submit a plan that describes how its program meets applicable requirements and must receive approval of the plan from the Centers for Medicare & Medicaid Services (CMS).

On August 17, 2007, CMS issued a letter purporting to clarify statutory and regulatory requirements related to preventing SCHIP substitution for other insurance coverage in states wishing to cover children with effective family incomes in excess of 250 percent of the federal poverty level (FPL). The letter indicates that CMS will apply measures identified in the letter to state proposals to cover these children, as well as to states that already cover them, and may take corrective action against states that fail to adopt the measures within 12 months.

In response to a request from the Chairman of the Subcommittee on Health Care, Senate Committee on Finance, and a member of that Subcommittee, GAO considered whether the letter is a rule under the Congressional Review Act (the Review Act). This testimony is based on the resulting opinion, *Applicability of the Congressional Review Act to Letter on State Children's Health Insurance Program*, B-316048, April 17, 2008.

Mr. Chairman and Members of the Subcommittee:

We appreciate the opportunity to participate in today's hearing on the August 17, 2007, letter issued by the Centers for Medicare & Medicaid Services (CMS) on the State Children's Health Insurance Program (SCHIP). My testimony focuses on GAO's April 17, 2008, opinion, which addressed whether the CMS letter is a rule for purposes of section 251 of the Contract with America Advancement Act of 1996,[1] commonly referred to as the Congressional Review Act (the Review Act).[2] In that opinion, we concluded that the letter is a rule under the Review Act, which, consistent with the Act's requirements, must be submitted to Congress and the Comptroller General before it can take effect.

BACKGROUND

SCHIP finances health care to low-income, uninsured children whose family incomes exceed the eligibility limits under their state's Medicaid program, but who cannot afford other health insurance coverage.[3] To participate in SCHIP, a state must submit a plan that describes how its program meets applicable requirements and must receive approval of the plan from CMS.[4] States are required to amend their plans to reflect changes in federal law, regulation, or policy, and changes in the operation of their programs, including, for example, changes in eligibility criteria or benefits.[5]

State SCHIP programs are subject to a number of statutory provisions that are designed to ensure that SCHIP coverage does not become a substitute for other public or private coverage. For example, a state plan must describe the procedures used to ensure that coverage under the plan does not substitute for coverage under group health plans, generally referred to as "crowd out."[6] Regulations promulgated by CMS require states to adopt "reasonable procedures" to prevent crowd out.[7] Since CMS promulgated the regulations in 2001, states have adopted a number of different measures to prevent crowd out, which CMS has approved.

In its August 17 letter, CMS purports to clarify the statutory and regulatory requirements concerning prevention of crowd out for states wishing to provide SCHIP coverage to children with effective family incomes in excess of 250 percent of the federal poverty level (FPL) and identifies a number of particular measures that these states should adopt. For example, according to the letter, states should impose cost sharing in approximation to the cost of private coverage and establish a minimum of a 1-year period of uninsurance for individuals prior to receiving coverage. In addition, the letter states that CMS will seek a number of assurances from states, including an assurance that the state has enrolled at least 95 percent of the children in the state with family incomes below 200 percent of the FPL who are eligible for SCHIP or Medicaid. The letter indicates that CMS will apply the measures to states' proposals to cover children with effective family incomes in excess of 250 percent of the FPL, as well as to states that already cover such children. According to the letter, CMS may take corrective action against states that fail to adopt the identified measures within 12 months.

DISCUSSION

The definition of "rule" in the Review Act incorporates by reference the definition of "rule" in the Administrative Procedure Act (APA), with some exceptions. To determine whether the August 17 letter is a rule under the Review Act, we thus considered whether the letter is a rule under the APA and whether it falls within any of the exceptions contained in the Review Act.[8] Section 55 1(4) of the APA defines the term rule in pertinent part as "[t]he whole or a part of an agency statement of general or particular applicability and future effect designed to implement, interpret, or prescribe law or policy or describing the organization, procedure, or practice requirements of an agency . . . ."[9] This definition of rule has been said to include "nearly every statement an agency may make."[10]

Agency statements that create binding legal norms—those that, for example, grant rights, impose obligations, or affect private interests—are rules under the APA.[11] These rules—usually called legislative rules— generally must be promulgated through notice and comment rulemaking procedures under 5 U.S.C. § 553.

Courts have found that other agency pronouncements also are rules as defined in 5 U.S.C. § 551, even if they do not create binding legal norms and are not subject to notice and comment rulemaking requirements under section 553. For example, agency guidance documents and manuals have been held to be rules.[12] Agency documents that clarify or explain existing legal requirements also have been held to be rules.[13] Whether a particular agency pronouncement is a rule under section 551, therefore, does not turn on whether the rule is subject to notice and comment rulemaking requirements under section 553. Legislative history of the Review Act confirms that it is intended to include almost all rules that an agency issues and reaches far more than those that must be promulgated according to the notice and comment requirements of section 553.[14]

The APA definition of rule includes three elements relevant to our consideration of the SCHIP letter: an agency statement is a rule if it is of general applicability; of future effect; and designed to implement, interpret, or prescribe law or policy. We concluded that the August 17 letter meets these criteria. We found the letter to be of general, rather than particular, applicability since it extends to all states that seek to enroll children with effective family incomes exceeding 250 percent of the FPL in their SCHIP programs, as well as to all states that have already enrolled such children.[15] In addition, we found it to be of future effect, that is, concerned with policy considerations for the future rather than the evaluation of past or present conduct.[16] Finally, the letter purports to clarify and explain the manner in which CMS applies statutory and regulatory requirements to states that want to extend coverage under their SCHIP programs to children with effective family incomes above 250 percent of the FPL and seeks to promote the implementation of statutory requirements applicable to state plans. Accordingly, we found that the letter is designed to implement, interpret, or prescribe law or policy.[17]

The history of the regulatory provision regarding substitution of coverage supported our view that the August 17 letter is a rule. In the preamble to the proposed rule to implement SCHIP, CMS indicated that it could not require states to adopt any particular measures to prevent substitution of coverage, stating that it did not have a statutory or empirical basis for doing so.[18] CMS confirmed this interpretation in a final rule.[19] In its August 17 letter, however, CMS states that its experience and information derived from the operation of SCHIP programs have made it clear that the potential for substitution is greater at higher income levels, and states seeking to expand their SCHIP populations should implement specific strategies as "reasonable procedures" to prevent substitution of coverage (for example, a minimum 1-year period of uninsurance before receiving SCHIP coverage). Thus, the letter amounts to a marked departure from the agency's settled interpretation of the regulation regarding substitution of coverage, and case law indicates that such a change may be made only by rule.[20]

We also found it significant that CMS had expressly relied on the letter to disapprove a state's request to amend its SCHIP plan to cover children with family incomes above 250 percent of the FPL. Specifically, in April 2007, the state of New York requested permission from CMS to amend its SCHIP plan to provide coverage to children with family incomes up to 400 percent of the FPL. CMS denied New York's request with specific reliance on the terms of the August 17 letter. For example, CMS indicated that the state failed to provide assurances that it had enrolled at least 95 percent of the children with family incomes below 200 percent of the FPL and that "as outlined in an August 17, 2007, letter, . . . such assurances are necessary to ensure that expansion to higher income populations does not interfere with the effective and efficient provision of child health assistance." CMS also cited the fact that the state's proposal did not include a 1-year period of uninsurance for populations over 250 percent of the FPL. CMS concluded stating that its disapproval was "consistent with the August 17, 2007, letter to State Health Officials discussing how . . . existing statutory and regulatory requirements should be applied to all States expanding SCHIP effective eligibility levels above 250 percent of the FPL." This application of the letter to deny New York's proposed plan amendment served to confirm that the letter has binding effect and is, therefore, a rule.[21]

During the course of our work, we requested the views of the General Counsel of the Department of Health and Human Services on whether the August 17 letter is a rule for purposes of the Review Act.[22] The response from the Director of the Center for Medicaid and State Operations within CMS did not directly address that issue. CMS indicated, however, that the letter is a "general statement of policy that announces the course which the agency intends to follow in adjudications concerning compliance with requirements already set forth in regulations." The agency also referred us to a document prepared by the Department of Justice, which asserted that the August 17 letter was a general statement of policy.

As discussed in our opinion, general statements of policy would appear to fit squarely within the definition of rule in the APA since they advise the public prospectively of the manner in which an agency proposes to exercise a discretionary power or what the agency will propose as policy.[23] Further, courts have referred to them as rules.[24] While some cases seem to suggest that general statements of policy are not rules under the APA,[25] the better reading of these cases, in our view, is that statements of policy are rules under section 551 of the APA but not the type of rules for which the APA requires notice and comment procedures because they are tentative statements of future intent and by their nature do not have the force of law.

Further, even if these cases are read to mean that general statements of policy are not rules under the APA, we found that the August 17 letter does not have the characteristics of a general statement of policy identified in case law. One case provided a particularly useful explanation of the type of language typically found in an agency general statement of policy. In *Pacific Gas and Electric Co. v. Federal Power Commission*,[26] the United States Court of Appeals for the District of Columbia Circuit considered a pronouncement, styled a "statement of policy," that expressed the Federal Power Commission's (Commission) view of how deliveries of natural gas should be prioritized during periods of shortage. The court held that the pronouncement was a general statement of policy, noting the tentative nature of the statement and the Commission's acknowledgment that any particular decisions on curtailment could only be made in further proceedings. Among other things, the court found it significant that the statement indicated it was the curtailment policy that the Commission "proposes to implement" and the "plan preferred by the Commission," which "will serve as a guide in other proceedings." In addition, the Commission itself intended the statement only "to state initial guidelines as a means of facilitating curtailment planning and the adjudication of curtailment cases." In effect, the Commission statement was a starting point to frame consideration of future proposals.

We analyzed CMS's August 17 letter under the criteria used by the court to determine that the Commission's pronouncement was simply a statement of policy and concluded that the letter does not meet the criteria. The specific measures identified in the letter are not characterized as "proposals" or measures that are under development or to be implemented or adopted by later action; on the contrary, the letter sets forth specific strategies that states seeking to expand their SCRIP populations should implement as "reasonable procedures" to prevent substitution of coverage. In addition, the letter contains no indication that the strategies are only guidelines that may or may not be applied in subsequent proceedings or express reference to exceptions in particular instances. Finally, the time frame specified in the letter for states to conform to the CMS "review strategy" evidences the agency's intention to give the letter present and binding effect; if the letter were simply precatory or tentative in nature, then there would be no need to establish a deadline by which states would need to implement the measures in the letter or face the possibility of a corrective action by the agency.[27] Because the letter establishes a deadline by which "affected States" need to implement its measures or face the possibility of corrective action, we found that it evidences little, if any, of the tentativeness that is the hallmark of a policy statement.

In addition to the particular language of a statement, courts look to an agency's actions in relation to the statement to determine whether it is a general statement of policy. As a number of courts have noted, a critical test of whether a rule is a general statement of policy is its practical effect in subsequent administrative proceedings. If the agency relies solely on the pronouncement itself to determine rights and obligations of others, the agency has treated the policy statement as if it were a binding rule, not a general statement of policy.[28] CMS's express reliance on the August 17 letter to deny the state of New York's request to amend its SCHIP plan led us to conclude that the letter is not a policy statement. This conclusion was reinforced by our observation that the August 17 letter reflects a significant change in the agency's settled interpretation of 42 C.F.R. § 457.805, which policy statements by their nature do not do.[29]

CONCLUSION

We concluded that the August 17, 2007, letter to state health officials is a rule for the purpose of the Review Act on the grounds that it is a statement of general applicability and future effect designed to implement, interpret, or prescribe law or policy with regard to SCHIP. Furthermore, we found that the letter does not come within any of the exceptions to the definition of rule contained in the Review Act. We expressed no opinion on the applicability of any other legal requirements, including, but not limited to, notice and comment rulemaking requirements under the APA, or whether the August 17 letter would be a valid interpretation of statutes or regulations.

Mr. Chairman, this concludes my prepared statement. I would be happy to respond to any questions that you or other Members of the Subcommittee may have.

REFERENCES

[1] Pub. L. No. 104-121, § 251, 110 Stat. 847, 868-74, *codified at* 5 U.S.C. §§ 801-808.

[2] Applicability of the Congressional Review Act to Letter on State Children's Health *Insurance Program,* B-316048, April 17, 2008. The opinion is available at http://gao.gov/decisions/other/other.htm.

[3] *See* 42 U.S.C. § 1397aa.

[4] 42 U.S.C. § 1397aa(b). The authority vested in the Secretary of Health and Human Services to approve and disapprove SCHIP state plans and plan amendments has been delegated to the Administrator of CMS. State Child Health; Implementing Regulations for the State *Children's Health Insurance Program,* 64 Fed. Reg. 60882, 60895 (Nov. 8, 1999) (proposed rule).

[5] 42 C.F.R. § 457.60.

[6] 42 U.S.C. § 1397bb(b)(3)(C).

[7] 42 C.F.R. § 457.805.

[8] The Review Act excepts the following from its definition of rule: (1) rules of particular applicability, including a rule that approves or prescribes for future application rates, wages, prices, services, or allowances therefor, corporate or financial structures, reorganizations, mergers, or acquisitions thereof, or accounting practices or disclosures bearing on any of the foregoing; (2) rules relating to agency management or personnel; and (3) rules of agency organization, procedure, or practice that do not substantially affect the rights or obligations of non-agency parties. 5 U.S.C. § 804(3). As discussed below, the letter is not a statement of particular applicability; rather, it substantially affects all states that seek to cover children with effective family incomes in excess of 250 percent of the FPL, as well as those states that already cover these children. The letter does not relate to agency management or personnel, and it does not relate to "agency organization, procedure, or practice" with no substantial effect on non-agency parties. Accordingly, we concluded that none of these three exceptions apply to the August 17 letter.

[9] 5 U.S.C. § 551(4).

[10] *Batterton v. Marshall*, 648 F.2d 694, 700 (D.C. Cir. 1980) (*citing* 5 U.S.C. § 551(4)).

[11] *Id.* at 700-02.

[12] *See Reno v. Koray*, 515 U.S. 50, 60–61 (1995) (internal agency guideline was a rule under the APA); *Shalala v. Guernsey Memorial Hospital*, 514 U.S. 87, 99–100 (1995) (provision of the Medicare Provider Reimbursement Manual was a rule under the APA); *Appalachian Power Co. v. Environmental Protection Agency,* 208 F.3d 1015, 1021–22 (D.C. Cir. 2000) (agency guidance document can be rule under the APA); *Professionals and Patients for Customized Care v. Shalala*, 56 F.3d 592, 601–02 (5th Cir. 1995) (FDA Compliance Policy Guide was a rule, but was exempt from notice and comment procedures as a statement of policy or interpretative rule).

[13] See, e.g., A.D. Transport Express, Inc. v. United States, 290 F.3d 761, 768 (6th Cir. 2002) (order explaining agency regulation is an interpretative rule under the APA); Guardian Federal Savings and Loan Ass'n v. Federal Savings and Loan Insurance Corp., 589 F.2d 658, 664 (D.C. Cir. 1978) (agency statements that clarify laws or regulations are rules under the APA).

[14] 142 Cong. Rec. H3005 (daily ed. Mar. 28, 1996) (statement of Rep. McIntosh) (noting that although agency interpretive rules, general statements of policy, guideline documents, and agency policy and procedure manuals may not

be subject to notice and comment requirements, they are covered under the congressional review provisions of the new chapter 8 of title 5).

[15] *Cf. U.S. Dep't of Justice, Attorney General's Manual on the Administrative Procedure Act* 13 (1947) (the term rule includes statements of particular applicability applying either to a class or to a single person).

[16] *See Bowen v. Georgetown University Hospital,* 488 U.S. 204, 216 (1988) (Scalia, J., concurring) ("future effect" means that agency statement will have legal consequences for the future); *see also U.S. Dep't of Justice, Attorney General's Manual on the Administrative Procedure Act* at 14 (rulemaking regulates the future conduct of either groups of persons or a single person and is essentially legislative in nature because it operates in the future and is primarily concerned with policy considerations, while adjudication is concerned with the determination of past and present rights and liabilities).

[17] *See A.D. Transport Express, Inc.*, 290 F.3d at 768 (order explaining agency regulation is an interpretative rule under the APA); *Guardian Federal Savings and Loan Ass'n*, 589 F.2d at 664 (agency statements that clarify laws or regulations are rules under the APA).

[18] 64 Fed. Reg. at 60921-22.

[19] See State Child Health; Implementing Regulations for the State Children's Health Insurance Program, 66 Fed. Reg. 2490, 2601-05 (Jan. 11, 2001) (final rule).

[20] *See SBC Inc. v. Federal Communications Commission,* 414 F.3d 486, 498 (3d Cir. 2005) (if agency's present interpretation of regulation is a fundamental modification of previous interpretation, the modification can only be accomplished through notice and comment rulemaking); *Shell Offshore Inc. v. Babbitt,* 238 F.3d 622, 629 (5th Cir. 2001) (settled policy of an agency is binding on the agency and may be changed only through a rule); *Alaska Professional Hunters Ass'n v. Federal Aviation Administration*, 177 F.3d 1030, 1033-34 (D.C. Cir. 1999) (an agency is bound by settled interpretation given to its own regulation that agency can change only by rulemaking).

[21] *See Appalachian Power Co.,* 208 F.3d at 1020-2 1 (if an agency treats a pronouncement as if it were controlling, if it bases enforcement actions on the policies in the document, and if it leads private parties or states to believe they must comply with the pronouncement's terms, it is a rule); *McLouth Steel Products Corp. v. Thomas*, 838 F.2d 1317, 1321 (D.C. Cir. 1988) (because agency used policy statement to determine regulated entities' obligations, policy statement is, therefore, a rule).

[22] In documents filed in related litigation, the Department of Justice has characterized the August 17 letter as a rule. *See New York v. United States Dep't of Health and Human Services,* No. 07 Civ. 08621 (S.D.N.Y. filed Oct. 4, 2007) (Def's Mem. Supp. Mot. Dismiss, p. 33).

[23] See U.S. Dep't of Justice, Attorney General's Manual on the Administrative Procedure Act at 30, n. 3.

[24] *See, e.g., Chrysler v. Brown,* 441 U.S. 281, 301 (1979) ("the central distinction among agency regulations found in the APA is that between 'substantive rules' on the one hand and 'interpretive rules, general statements of policy, or rules of agency organization, procedure, or practice' on the other"); *Noel v. Chapman,* 508 F.2d 1023, 1030 (2d Cir. 1975) (general statement of policy is a rule directed at agency staff on how it will perform discretionary function); *Guardian Federal Savings and Loan Ass'n,* 589 F.2d at 666 (describing test for determining whether "a rule is a general statement of policy").

[25] *See, e.g., Sugar Cane Growers Cooperative of Florida v. Veneman,* 289 F.3d 89, 95 (D.C. Cir. 2002) (some agency pronouncements lack the firmness of a prescribed standard to be considered rules); *Syncor International Corp. v. Shalala,* 127 F.3d 90, 94 (D.C. Cir. 1997) (the primary distinction between a rule and a general statement of policy is whether the agency intends to bind itself to a legal position); *Pacific Gas and Electric Co. v. Federal Power Commission,* 506 F.2d 33, 37 (D.C. Cir. 1974) (suggesting that policy statements are not rules under the APA).

[26] 506 F.2d 33 (D.C. Cir. 1974).

[27] *Cf. Community Nutrition Institute v. Young*, 818 F.2d 943, 947 (D.C. Cir. 1987) (agency pronouncement instructing regulated entities to obtain "exception" from standard in announcement indicated pronouncement was intended to be binding).

[28] *See Public Citizen, Inc. v. United States Nuclear Regulatory Commission,* 940 F.2d 679, 682-83 (D.C. Cir. 1991) (courts look to agency's actual application of statement to determine its nature if language and context of agency statement are not conclusive); *Guardian Federal Savings and Loan Ass'n,* 589 F.2d at 666 (in subsequent administrative proceeding, agency cannot claim that prior statement of policy itself resolves contested issues).

[29] *See Syncor International Corp.,* 127 F.3d at 94 (a general statement of policy does not impose, elaborate, or interpret a legal norm, but explains the agency's manner of enforcing the existing legal norm).

In: Revisiting and Evaluating the Congressional... ISBN: 978-1-60692-687-1
Editor: K. R. Williamson, pp. 95-103

Chapter 4

FEDERAL RULEMAKING: PERSPECTIVES ON 10 YEARS OF CONGRESSIONAL REVIEW ACT IMPLEMENTATION*

J. Christopher Mihm

WHAT GAO FOUND

CRA gives Congress an opportunity to review most rules before they take effect and to disapprove those found to be too burdensome, excessive, inappropriate, duplicative, or otherwise objectionable. Under CRA, two types of rules, major and nonmajor, must be submitted to both Houses of Congress and GAO before they can take effect. The Office of Information and Regulatory Affairs (OIRA) of the Office of Management and Budget specifies which rules are designated as major rules based on criteria set out in the CRA. Major rules cannot be effective until 60 days after publication in the *Federal Register* or submission to Congress and GAO, whichever is later. Congress may disapprove agencies' rules by introducing a resolution of disapproval that, if adopted by both Houses of Congress and signed by the President, can nullify an agency's rule. Members of Congress seldom have attempted to use this process.

GAO's role under CRA is to provide Congress with a report on each major rule concerning GAO's assessment of the promulgating federal agency's compliance with

---

* This is an edited, excerpted and augmented edition of a United States Government Accountability Office publication, Report GAO-06-601T, dated March 30, 2006.

the procedural steps required by various acts and executive orders governing the regulatory process. GAO compiles information on the rules it receives under CRA in a database containing basic information about major and nonmajor rules. GAO also conducts an annual review to determine whether all final rules covered by the Act and published in the *Federal Register* have been filed with the Congress and GAO. Although we reported that agencies' compliance with CRA requirements was inconsistent during the first years after CRA's enactment, compliance improved over time.

There have been a limited number of CRA joint resolutions, but the benefits of compiling and making information available on potential federal actions should not be underestimated. The procedures for congressional disapproval also may have some deterrent effect. Efforts to enhance presidential oversight of agencies' rulemaking appear to have been more significant and widely employed in recent years than similar efforts to enhance congressional oversight. Some recent legislative proposals have focused on expanding the information and analysis available to Congress on pending rules, while others focus on enhancing the mechanisms that Congress could employ for its own review—and potential disapproval—of agencies' rules.

Facts on CRA since Its Enactment on March 29, 1996

- 37 Joint Resolutions of Disapproval introduced affecting 28 rules
- 1 rule nullified by Congress through Joint Resolution procedures
- 610 major rules received and reported on by GAO
- 41,218 nonmajor rules entered into GAO database
- About 200 nonmajor rules per year not filed with GAO
- All 610 major rules filed with GAO in a timely fashion
- 71 of 610 major rules—effective date not delayed for required 60 days

WHY GAO DID THIS STUDY

This year marks the 10th anniversary of the Congressional Review Act (CRA). Congressional oversight of rulemaking using the CRA can be an important and useful tool for monitoring the regulatory process and balancing and accommodating the concerns of American citizens and businesses with the effects of federal agencies' rules. This statement provides an overview of the purpose and provisions of CRA; GAO's role and activities in fulfilling its responsibilities under the Act; and trends on CRA within the broader context of developments in presidential and congressional oversight of federal agencies' rulemaking.

Mr. Chairman and Members of the Subcommittee:

I am pleased to appear before you today on the 10th anniversary of the enactment of the Congressional Review Act (CRA).[1] As you know, CRA was enacted to ensure that Congress has an opportunity to review, and possibly reject, rules before they become effective. Under CRA, two types of rules, major and nonmajor, must be submitted to both Houses of Congress and GAO before they can take effect. We are required to provide Congress with a report on each major rule concerning our assessment of the promulgating federal agency's compliance with the procedural steps required by various acts and executive orders governing the regulatory process.

Over the past 10 years, agencies have submitted information on thousands of rules as required by the CRA. Although we generally found that agencies complied with CRA's requirements, one main area of noncompliance has been that agencies have not always delayed the effective date of their major rules for 60 days, as required by the Act. While considerable information on agencies' rules has been reported under CRA, to date Congress has used the Act to disapprove only one rule, the Department of Labor's rule on ergonomics in 2001. In contrast, our reviews indicated that efforts to increase presidential influence and authority over the regulatory process have become more significant and widely used over the years.

In my statement today, I will focus on three topics. First, I will provide a quick overview of the purpose and provisions of CRA. Second, I will discuss GAO's role in fulfilling its responsibilities under the Act and summarize our CRA activities over the years. Finally, I will address CRA within the broader context of developments in presidential and congressional oversight of federal agencies' rulemaking. My statement is based on our activities and observations implementing our responsibilities under CRA over the past decade and our related body of work reviewing federal regulatory issues.

Overview of CRA Purpose, Procedures, and Requirements

Congressional oversight of rulemaking using the CRA can be an important and useful tool for monitoring the regulatory process and balancing and accommodating the concerns of American citizens and businesses with the effects of federal agencies' rules. As we noted early in the implementation of CRA, it is important to assure that executive branch agencies are responsive to citizens and businesses about the reach, cost, and impact of regulations, without compromising the statutory mission given to those agencies.[2] CRA seeks to accomplish this by giving Congress an opportunity to review most rules before they take effect and to disapprove those found to be too burdensome, excessive, inappropriate, duplicative, or otherwise objectionable.

With certain exceptions, CRA applies to most rules issued by federal agencies, including the independent regulatory agencies.[3] Under CRA, two types of rules, major and nonmajor, must be submitted to both Houses of Congress and GAO before they can take effect. CRA defines a "major" rule as one which results or is likely to result in (1) an annual effect on the economy of $100 million or more; (2) a major increase in costs or prices for consumers, individual industries, government agencies, or geographic regions; or (3) significant adverse effects on competition, employment, investment, productivity, innovation, or on the ability of U.S.-based enterprises to compete with foreign-based enterprises in domestic and export markets. CRA specifies that the determination of what rules are major is to be made by the Office of Information and Regulatory Affairs (OIRA) of the Office of Management and Budget (OMB). Major rules cannot be effective until 60 days after publication in the Federal Register or submission to Congress and GAO, whichever is later. Nonmajor rules become effective when specified by the agency, but not before they are filed with Congress and GAO.

CRA established a procedure by which members of Congress may disapprove agencies' rules by introducing a resolution of disapproval that, if adopted by both Houses of Congress and signed by the President, can nullify an agency's rule. If such a resolution becomes law, the rule then cannot take effect or continue in effect. In addition, CRA prohibits an agency from reissuing such a rule in substantially the same form, or a new rule that is substantially the same as the disapproved rule, unless the reissued or new rule is specifically authorized by a law enacted after the date of the joint resolution disapproving the original rule. Members of Congress seldom have attempted to use this disapproval process. Over the past decade, 37 joint resolutions of disapproval have been introduced regarding 28 rules. Only once has Congress used this disapproval process to nullify a rule, when it disapproved the Department of Labor's rule on ergonomics in 2001.[4]

GAO's Role and Activities under CRA

GAO's only stated role under CRA is to provide Congress with a report on each major rule concerning GAO's assessment of the promulgating federal agency's "compliance with the procedural steps" required by various acts and executive orders governing the regulatory process. These include preparation of a cost-benefit analysis, when required, and compliance with the Regulatory Flexibility Act, the Unfunded Mandates Reform Act of 1995 (UMRA), the Administrative Procedure Act (APA), the Paperwork Reduction Act, and Executive Order 12866. GAO's report must be sent to the congressional committees of jurisdiction within 15 calendar days of the publication of the rule or submission of the rule by the agency, whichever is later. While the CRA is silent with regard to GAO's role concerning nonmajor rules, we found that basic information about those rules also should be collected in a manner that can be of use to Congress and the public.

To compile information on all the rules submitted to us under CRA, we established a database, available to the public on the Internet.[5] Our database gathers basic information about the 15–20 major and nonmajor rules that we receive each day, including the title, the agency, the Regulation Identification Number, the type of rule, the proposed effective date, the date published in the Federal Register, the congressional review trigger date, and any joint resolutions of disapproval that may have been introduced. We created a standardized submission form available on the Internet, which is used by almost all the agencies, to allow more consistent information collection. Since CRA was enacted on March 29, 1996, we have received and submitted timely reports on 610 major rules and entered 41,218 nonmajor rules into the database.[6]

As noted earlier, before a rule can become effective, it must be filed in accordance with CRA. We conduct an annual review to determine whether all final rules covered by the Act and published in the Federal Register have been filed with the Congress and us. We perform the review to both verify the accuracy of our database and to ascertain the degree of agency compliance with CRA. We forward a list of unfiled rules to OIRA for their handling, and, in the past, they have disseminated the list to the agencies, most of which file the rules or offer an explanation of why they do not believe a rule is covered by CRA.

Although we reported that agencies' compliance with CRA requirements was inconsistent during the first years after CRA's enactment, compliance improved over time. In general, we have found the degree of compliance to have remained fairly constant, with roughly 200 nonmajor rules per year not filed with our office. In the 10 years since CRA was enacted, all major rules have been filed in a timely fashion.

In the past 10 years, we also have issued eight opinions regarding what constitutes a "rule" under CRA in response to requests from congressional committees and members concerning various agency pronouncements and memorandums. CRA contains a broad definition of the term "rule," including more than the usual notice and comment rulemakings published in the Federal Register under APA. Under CRA, "rule" means the whole or part of an agency statement of general applicability and future effect designed to implement, interpret, or prescribe law or policy. For example, in 1996 we concluded that a memorandum issued by the Secretary of Agriculture in connection with the Emergency Salvage Timber Sale Program constituted a rule under CRA and should have been submitted to Congress and GAO before it could become effective.[7] Similarly, in 2001, we concluded that a Fish and Wildlife Service Record of Decision entitled "Trinity River Mainstem Fishery Restoration" was a rule covered by CRA.[8] We believe these opinions have strengthened the reach of CRA by insuring compliance with the main thrust of the Act, which was to insure that agency actions, whether labeled a "rule" by the agency or not, are subject to congressional review. We have noted that certain congressional committees, such as the Joint Committee on Taxation, were taking an active role in overseeing agency compliance with CRA. As a result, for example, Internal Revenue Service procedures, rulings, regulations, notices, and announcements are forwarded as CRA submittals.

The one major area of noncompliance with the requirements of the Act has been that agencies have not always delayed the effective date of major rules for 60 days as required by the Act.[9] Agencies have filed 610 major rules with our office, and, for 71 of those rules, the agencies did not delay the effective date for the required 60 days.

One reason for noncompliance with the 60-day delay is that the agencies have misapplied the "good cause" exception which waives the delay of the rule if it would be impracticable, unnecessary, or contrary to the public interest.[10] Since the enactment of CRA, our office has consistently held that the "good cause" exception is only available if a notice of proposed rulemaking was not published and public comments were not received.[11] Many agencies, following a notice of proposed rulemaking and receipt of comments, have stated in the preamble to the final major rule that "good cause" existed for not providing the 60-day delay.

The other reason for noncompliance is that the statute that an agency is implementing by issuing the final major rule contains a date by which the Secretary or Administrator must issue the regulation, and the date, in many instances, does not permit the 60-day delay. However, the CRA states that it shall apply notwithstanding any other provision of law.[12]

TRENDS IN PRESIDENTIAL AND CONGRESSIONAL REVIEW OF RULEMAKING

Agencies and GAO have provided Congress a considerable amount of information about forthcoming rules in response to CRA. The limited number of CRA joint resolutions introduced might suggest that this information generates little additional oversight of rulemaking. However, as we found in our review of the information generated on federal mandates under UMRA, the benefits of compiling and making information available on potential federal actions should not be underestimated.[13] Further, as we also found regarding UMRA, the availability of procedures for congressional disapproval may have some deterrent effect. The Congressional Research Service has reported that several rules have been affected by the presence of the review mechanism, suggesting that the CRA review scheme has had some influence.

Still, as I noted in my testimony before this Subcommittee last November, efforts to enhance presidential oversight of agencies' rulemaking appear to have been more significant and widely employed in recent years than similar efforts to enhance congressional oversight.[14] In particular, our reviews have noted the growing influence and authority of OIRA in the oversight of the regulatory process.[15] Some of this increased activity reflects administration initiatives, but it also includes some new responsibilities assigned by Congress through statute, such as the requirement for OMB to issue governmentwide guidance to implement the Information Quality Act.[16]

In contrast, there does not appear to have been a similar expansion of direct congressional influence and authority over the regulatory process, although bills have been introduced over the years to enhance the mechanisms available for congressional oversight of agencies' rulemaking. Some recent legislative proposals have focused on expanding the information and analysis available to Congress on pending rules, while others focus on enhancing the mechanisms that Congress could employ for its own review—and potential disapproval—of agencies' rules.

As the major example of the first category of proposals, Congress passed the Truth in Regulating Act (TIRA) in 2000 to provide a mechanism for it to obtain more information about certain rules.[17] In contrast to the essentially procedural reviews that GAO now conducts under CRA, TIRA contemplated a 3-year pilot project during which GAO would perform independent evaluations of "economically significant" agency rules when requested by a chairman or ranking member of a committee of jurisdiction of either House of Congress. However, during the 3-year period contemplated for the pilot project, Congress did not enact any specific appropriation to cover TIRA evaluations, as called for in the Act, and the authority for the 3-year pilot project expired on January 15, 2004. Therefore, we have no information on the potential effectiveness of this mechanism.

Congress has considered reauthorizing TIRA, and we have strongly urged that any reauthorization of TIRA continue to contain language requiring a specific annual appropriation for GAO before we are required to undertake independent evaluations of major rulemakings. Such an expansion of GAO's current lines of business without additional dedicated resources would pose a serious problem for us, especially in light of what will likely be increasing budgetary constraints in the years ahead. It would also likely serve to adversely affect our ability to provide the same level of service to the Congress in connection with our existing statutory authorities. We have also recommended that TIRA evaluations be conducted under a pilot project basis.

Members of Congress have also introduced several bills over the past year that would provide additional mechanisms for direct review and approval (or disapproval) of agencies' rules.[18] Some of these proposals would modify how Congress reviews information submitted under CRA and how the disapproval procedures would work. These bills could, for example, create a joint committee that would be tasked with reviewing all rules to determine whether a disapproval resolution under CRA should be introduced. We have conducted no work that would provide information on the potential effectiveness of such changes.

Mr. Chairman, this concludes my prepared statement. Once again, I appreciate the opportunity to testify on these important issues. I would be pleased to address any questions you or other Members of the Subcommittee might have at this time.

If additional information is needed regarding this testimony, please contact J. Christopher Mihm, Managing Director, Strategic Issues, at (202) 512-6806 or mihmj@gao.gov.

REFERENCES

[1] U.S.C. §§ 801-808. CRA was enacted as Subtitle E of the Small Business Regulatory Enforcement Fairness Act of 1996 (SBREFA), Pub. L. No. 104-121, on March 29, 1996.

[2] GAO, *Congressional Review Act*, GAO/T-OGC-97-29 (Washington, D.C.: Mar. 6, 1997).

[3] In addition to some general exceptions, such as one regarding any rule relating to agency management or personnel, CRA does not apply to any rule promulgated under the Telecommunications Act of 1996 and the amendments made by that Act. Nor does CRA apply to rules that concern monetary policy proposed or implemented by the Board of Governors of the Federal Reserve System or the Federal Open Market Committee.

[4] Pub. L. No. 107-5, 115 Stat. 7 (Mar. 20, 2001).

[5] GAO's Federal Rules Database is publicly available at www.gao.gov under the "Legal Products" link. The reports we prepare on major rules under CRA are also available on that site.

[6] Number of major and nonmajor rules are as of March 24, 2006.

[7] See B-274505, Sept. 16, 1996.

[8] See B-287557, May 14, 2001.

[9] 5 U.S.C. § 801(a)(3)(A).

[10] 5 U.S.C. § 808(2).

[11] See B-275549; B-275552, Dec. 9, 1996.

[12] 5 U.S.C. § 806(a).

[13] See GAO, Unfunded Mandates: Analysis of Reform Act Coverage, GAO-04-637 (Washington, D.C.: May 12, 2004) and Unfunded Mandates: Views Vary About Reform Act's Strengths, Weaknesses, and Options for Improvement, GAO-05-454 (Washington, D.C.: Mar. 31, 2005).

[14] See GAO, Federal Rulemaking: Past Reviews and Emerging Trends Suggest Issues That Merit Congressional Attention, GAO-06-228T (Washington, D.C.: Nov. 1, 2005).

[15] See GAO, Rulemaking: OMB's Role in Reviews of Agencies' Draft Rules and the Transparency of Those Reviews, GAO-03-929 (Washington, D.C.: Sept. 22, 2003).

[16] The Information Quality Act is also known as the Data Quality Act. Consolidated Appropriations Act, 2001, Pub. L. No. 106-554, 114 Stat. 2763, 2763A-153-54 (Dec. 21, 2000).

[17] Pub. L. No. 106-3 12, 114 Stat. 1248 (Oct. 17, 2000), 5 U.S.C. § 801 note.

[18] See, for example, H.R. 576, H.R. 931, and H.R. 3148.

In: Revisiting and Evaluating the Congressional… ISBN: 978-1-60692-687-1
Editor: K. R. Williamson, pp. 105-109

Chapter 5

CONGRESSIONAL REVIEW ACT*

Gary Kepplinger

Chairwoman Sanchez, Mr. Cannon, and Members of the Subcommittee:

I am pleased to submit this statement for the record on the Government Accountability Office's responsibilities under the Congressional Review Act (CRA), and our processes and experiences in carrying out these responsibilities. CRA was designed to give Congress an opportunity to review a rule before it takes effect and to disapprove any rule to which Congress objects through the passage of a joint resolution with presentment to the President.

Under CRA two types of rules, major and nonmajor, must be submitted to both Houses of Congress and GAO before either can take effect. 5 U.S.C. § 801(a)(1)(A). CRA defines a "major" rule as one which has resulted in or is likely to result in (1) an annual effect on the economy of $100 million or more; (2) a major increase in costs or prices for consumers, individual industries, government agencies, or geographic regions; or (3) significant adverse effects on competition, employment, investment, productivity, innovation, or on the ability of U.S.-based enterprises to compete with foreign-based enterprises in domestic and export markets. 5 U.S.C. § 804(2). CRA specifies that the determination of whether a rule is major is to be made by the Office of Information and Regulatory Affairs (OIRA) at the Office of Management and Budget (OMB). *Id.* Major rules cannot be effective until 60 days after publication in the

---

* This is an edited, excerpted and augmented edition of a United States Government Accountability Office publication, Report GAO-08-268T, dated November 6, 2007.

Federal Register or submission to Congress, whichever is later. 5 U.S.C. § 801(a)(3).[1] Nonmajor rules become effective when specified by the agency, but not before they are filed with the Congress. 5 U.S.C. § 801(a)(4).

GAO's primary role under CRA is to provide the Congress with a report on each major rule containing GAO's assessment of whether the promulgating federal agency's submissions to GAO indicate that it has complied with the procedural steps required by various acts and Executive Orders governing the regulatory process. 5 U.S.C. § 801(a)(2)(A). These steps include preparation of a cost-benefit analysis, where required, and compliance with the Regulatory Flexibility Act, the Unfunded Mandates Reform Act of 1995, the Administrative Procedure Act, the Paperwork Reduction Act, and Executive Order No. 12866. In addition, our Office provides a copy of each major rule to the interested audit or evaluation team within GAO toascertain if GAO has any work relevant to the rule which should be brought to the attention of the Congress. GAO's report must be sent to the congressional committees of jurisdiction within 15 calendar days.[2]

CRA is silent as to GAO's role relating to the nonmajor rules. However, since we began receiving rules from federal agencies under CRA in 1996 (Pub. L. No. 104-121, §§251-253, 110 Stat. 847, 868 (1996)), we have collected and made available to Congress and the public in a researchable database on our website certain basic information about major and nonmajor rules. This database contains information about the 10 rules we receive on average each day, including the title of the rule, the agency, the Regulation Identification Number,[3] the type of rule (major or nonmajor), the proposed effective date, the date published in the Federal Register, the congressional review trigger date, any joint resolutions of disapproval that may be enacted, and, in the case of major rules, a link to GAO's report on the rule. Since the enactment of CRA in 1996, through October 30, 2007, GAO has received 46,136 rules and of those 703 were major rules for which we prepared reports for Congress.

STANDARDIZED SUBMISSION FORM

GAO has developed for agencies a standardized submission form, which allows for more efficient processing of rules delivered under CRA. Agencies now submit a standardized "Submission of Federal Rules under the Congressional Review Act" form with each rule submitted to GAO. The form includes the information required by CRA for agency reports accompanying submitted rules, such as the Department or Agency name, the title of the rule, the Rule Identification Number and whether or not the agency or OIRA considers the rule to be major. 5 U.S.C. §

801(a)(1)(A). For major rules, the agency indicates which acts and Executive orders the agency determined were relevant to the rule, and whether or not information regarding compliance with these acts and orders is included in the rule as submitted. The form is available on the GAO's website and may be submitted electronically. The form is also available on the section of the OIRA website that offers guidance and forms to federal agencies.[4]

GAO Receipt of Rules

Federal agencies may use a variety of means to submit rules and reports to GAO, including hand-delivery, postal mail, facsimile or electronic mail. GAO has been able to receive agency rules and reports electronically since 1999, although only a handful of agencies have used this method to transmit rules. Our conversations with agencies indicate that this is attributable, in part, to the fact that the House of Representatives and the Senate require paper copies to be submitted to fulfill the agency's obligation under CRA.

As noted earlier, a rule must be filed in accordance with CRA before it can become effective. 5 U.S.C. § 801(a)(1)(A). GAO has conducted yearly reviews to determine whether all final rules covered by CRA and published in the Federal Register were filed with GAO. We submit to OIRA each year a computer listing of rules we found published in the Federal Register the previous year that have not been filed with our Office. Additionally, GAO monitors the Federal Register daily for major rules under CRA to ensure that we receive all such rules. On the occasion that a major rule is published that has not been received by GAO, GAO promptly follows up with the agency to remind the agency of its responsibilities under CRA.

Sixty Day Delay

A consistent difficulty in implementing CRA has been the failure of some agencies to delay the effective date of major rules for 60 days as required by CRA. 5 U.S.C. § 801(a)(3)(A). In 2007, eight of the forty-three major rules we have reviewed to date have not allowed for the required 60-day delay. We find agencies are not budgeting enough time into their regulatory timetable to allow for the statutory delay. In one of these cases, the agency, Federal Energy Regulatory Commission, delayed the effective date of its rule to comply with CRA. 72 Fed. Reg. 31,452 (June 7, 2007).

CONCLUSION

We look forward to fulfilling GAO's continuing responsibilities under CRA and to working with the subcommittee in the future in its continued oversight of CRA processes and procedures.

APPENDIX: RULES RECEIVED UNDER CRA BY FISCAL YEAR

Fiscal Year	All Rules	Major Rules
1996[a]	2,059	35
1997	3,932	59
1998	4,746	70
1999	4,560	58
2000	4,619	65
2001	4,038	81
2002	3,736	52
2003	4,238	48
2004	4,139	63
2005	3,888	64
2006	3,058	54
2007	3,092	51
Total	46,105	700

Source: GAO Federal Rules Database.
[a] Reporting under the act began when CRA was passed on March 29, 1996.

REFERENCES

[1] Under CRA a delay in the effective date for rules does not apply in the case of rules related to hunting, fishing, or camping, or to rules where an agency finds "good cause." 5 U.S.C. § 808.

[2] In response to Congressional requests, we also have issued to the Congress eight legal opinions on whether or not an agency action is a rule as defined by CRA (B-292045, May 19, 2003; B-291906, February 28, 2003; B-287557, May 14, 2001; B-286338, October 17, 2000; B-281575, January 20, 1999; B-278224, November 10, 1997; B-275178, July 3, 1997; B-274505, September

16, 1996), and an additional opinion interpreting the 60-day delay period for major rules. B-289880, April 5, 2002.

[3] The Regulatory Information Service Center assigns a Regulation Identification Number (RIN) to identify each regulatory action listed in the Unified Agenda of Federal Regulatory and Deregulatory Actions. OMB has asked agencies to include RINs in the headings of their Rule and Proposed Rule documents when publishing them in the Federal Register, to make it easier for the public and agency officials to track the publication history of regulatory actions throughout their development.

[4] The form is available at http://www.whitehouse.gov/omb/inforeg/regpol-agency_review.html (last visited November 7, 2007).

INDEX

9

A

B

E

F

G

H

I

J

L

M

N

O

W